TARIKI

TARIKI

Embracing Despair, Discovering Peace

HIROYUKI ITSUKI

Translated by
JOSEPH ROBERT

KODANSHA
TOKYO • NEW YORK • LONDON

Kodansha Ltd.
12-21 Otowa 2-chome, Bunkyo-ku, Tokyo 112-8001

Kodansha America, Inc.
575 Lexington Avenue, New York, New York 10022

Published in 2001 by Kodansha Ltd.
Copyright © 2001 by Hiroyuki Itsuki
All rights reserved.

Originally published, in different form, in 1998 in Japanese, under the title *TARIKI* by Kodansha Ltd. Some portions were originally published as *Jinsei no mokuteki* and *Taiga no itteki* by Gento-sha.

English translation copyright © 2001 by Kodansha Ltd.

CIP data available

ISBN 4-06209-981-0
This book was edited by Kodansha America, Inc.

Printed in Japan

01 02 03 04 05   10 9 8 7 6 5 4 3 2 1

Contents

Acknowledgments

A certain writer once said, "Everyone but myself is a mentor." While writing this book, I often had the opportunity to reflect on the weight these words carry. It would be impossible to name all those who had an impact on my ideas. There are an infinite number of people I have learned from—either through their writings or through real-life encounters. Here, I will name and thank only those who have directly helped me complete this book.

First of all, I must thank Professor Joryu Chiba, my former mentor at Ryukoku University, who taught me that Buddhism is not only a faith, but also a philosophy as well as a subject of study. I am equally thankful to the Reverend Nobutaka Ota, who gave me the opportunity to come in contact with religion in daily life. This book was born due to my ties with the numerous people I met through these two gentlemen.

There are two people in the Japanese publishing industry who truly encouraged and supported me. They are Mrs. Sawako Noma, president of Kodansha (also the publisher of the Japanese edition), and Mr. Toru Kenjo, an outstanding editor and publisher of Gento-sha. It would have been impossible to publish this English edition without the steady encouragement from Mrs. Noma.

Upon publishing this book in the United States, I would like to express my heartfelt thanks to Ms. Chikako Noma, editor at Kodansha America, for her tireless efforts throughout all aspects of the process; to Ms. Deborah Baker, editor, for her constant dedication to this project; and to Mr. Toshio Toyoda of Kodansha who gave life to both the Japanese and English editions. Chikako has been a friend since her days as a college student, and now as an editor with an accomplished career in New York, she has enthusiastically moved this project along from editing the manuscript to the completion of the book. I feel that being blessed to work with such an editor must also be due to the power of *tariki*.

Most of all, I would like to acknowledge Mr. Joseph Robert who is the translator of the English edition; Ms. Eiko Ishioka, the art director who designed an artistic book based on our many years of friendship; Mr. Toshiya Masuda, the graphic designer; and my wife, Reiko Itsuki, for adding depth to my book with artwork that touches the innermost parts of the human soul. She is both an artist and a psychiatrist, and she has given great inspiration and encouragement to my creative activities as a writer for these thirty-five years. I offer my deepest gratitude to everybody mentioned here—this book was made possible by your support.

Hiroyuki Itsuki

Foreword

The Strange Feeling of Other Power

When I wake up in the middle of the night, I often find myself asking what it was that has kept me going up to now, that has kept me alive. Is there anything that I really believe in?

The troubles of daily life often attack in an uninterrupted flurry, one after another: health problems; the first signs of old age; all sorts of difficulties with work and relationships, with family or children. Anxiety and restlessness, self-hate and unfocused anger, apathy and resignation, mark our days. Our daily lives are a simmering stew of these ingredients, and sometimes I am impressed, in a rueful way, that I have kept going all these decades. Human beings are really very tough.

And then there are the larger crises that each of us faces in the course of our lives. These are events that overturn our whole world. We succumb to life-threatening illnesses. We lose our reputation, social standing, and work in a single blow. Our children suffer blows in their own lives and we find there is nothing we can do to alleviate their pain. There are times when we must face not just unemployment but personal bankruptcy. I think I can say that I have faced such crises far more frequently than those who were born and raised in my country's relatively stable period of postwar growth.

Of course, I've had a vague feeling that there is some kind of "Other Power" for a long time.

Because I lived through many hardships in my youth, I think I probably began to have some sense, some awareness, of the concept of this Other Power during those years. This is what I would like to explore in this book. *Tariki* is the Japanese word for Other Power.

Tariki is one of the most important concepts in Japanese Buddhism, one which first emerged during a period of tremendous upheaval and suffering in Japan, a time that called into question humanity's efforts to control its destiny. *Tariki* stands in contrast to "Self-Power," or *jiriki.* Since its beginnings in India, Buddhism has taught a long and arduous path of practice to reach enlightenment. This personal effort made to achieve enlightenment is a manifestation of Self-Power. *Tariki,* on the other hand, is the recognition of the great, all-encompassing power of the Other—in this case, the Buddha and his ability to enlighten us—and the simultaneous recognition of the individual's utter powerlessness in the face of the realities of the human condition. It is, in my opinion, a more realistic, more mature, and more quintessentially modern philosophy than Self-Power, and it is a philosophy that can be a great source of strength to live in our world today.

Let me first, however, tell you something about myself.

I. The Ultimate Negative Thinker

On Days When—for Some Reason—the Spirit Withers

I have considered suicide twice. The first time was during my second year in junior high school, and the second time was in my early thirties, just after I had begun my career as a writer.

On both occasions, as I recall, I considered the actual method I might use. I was in a state of deep desperation, obviously.

When I look back at those times from the relative serenity of old age, it seems strange to me that I could have been so desperate. Yet, I do not regard my brushes with suicide as signs of emotional instability. To contemplate suicide is natural enough, particularly at certain stages of life. Life experience can bring anyone to the precipice, especially in times of historical upheaval.

In fact, I would go so far as to say that this contemplation of suicide, the considered act of bringing death from the distant, rarely considered future into the dark present, was a very good thing for me. Nietzsche said that whatever doesn't kill you makes you stronger. Perhaps the same is true of human beings who have survived despair.

All of us live with death close, but silent, at our side, easy to ignore if we choose to. Suicide is not an aberration but a recognition and embrace of death, a hand extended to claim it. Tossing away one's life is as easy as turning to acknowledge our silent companion. Some, I'm sure, choose death for no reason other than that their lives become too much trouble. Yet, all of us exist on the edge of a precipice that separates life from death. Most of us, however, never look down.

When one begins to contemplate suicide, it is because one has come to feel that life is a trial, a burden. This feeling grows stronger, of course, as we age, but for many it begins at a young age. High school students, even elementary school students and younger children, sometimes suffer keenly the pain of living. Although there are more distractions later in life, people still feel that pain after graduating from college and finding a job, after marrying and having children. All of us have moments in our lives when we pause, sigh deeply, and ask ourselves if it is worthwhile to go on.

It would be wonderful if all of us had the talent to adopt a positive attitude toward everything in life, but this is not always so easy. During dark moments, our bodies feel limp and we experience an emotion that is difficult to put into words. One way to describe it is to say the spirit withers, as flowers and leaves wither when they lose water.

When the spirit falters, we are depressed and cease to care about anything that happens to us. Our limbs feel slow and heavy, and sometimes we feel as if our bodies are not our own. Sometimes all we want to do is sleep.

After my two encounters with suicidal thoughts, I approached life with greater vigor. Yet, as I enter my late sixties, these thoughts have returned, but in a manner that is different from before. I am able to contemplate them with more patience.

I have tried various methods to free myself from this state, but I have to admit that, in most cases, I haven't succeeded. There's nothing one can do but wait for time to solve the problem. The flow of time engulfs all, carrying one back into the dull repetition of the patterns of daily life. One can only wait. That, perhaps, is the true wisdom of life. I know that. I know it, but still it is very, very hard to get through those long, heavy hours, simply enduring, simply waiting for them to pass.

Life Is Continuous Suffering and Despair

Every one of us, in this brief interval of life, is going to experience this "withering of the spirit" that I have talked about. I can't help thinking, however, that this feeling is caused by our unconscious assumptions about and unrealistic expectations for our lives. The fact is, life is not just a pleasurable experience. Although the present generation has come to expect that every person has some sort of inalienable right to a pleasant, healthy, happy life, I believe that this expectation is not only a delusion but a grave error.

Long ago people used to describe life as a long, long journey on which we all carry a very heavy load. The passage of a mere three or four centuries isn't going to change the reality of human experience.

We may not live any longer at the whim of a feudal master, in imminent danger of famine or disaster, but what can protect us from our individual suffering, or from the problems of birth, old age, sickness, and death? The sufferings of the feudal era have been replaced by new sufferings, peculiar to our time. Loneliness and alienation are two such examples. To get angry and demand why this is so manifests our delusion, our expectation that the terms of our existence have been profoundly altered. More than a thousand years ago, Prince Shotoku died with the words "The world is false and empty." Who can say whose time, his or ours, is more filled with pain and suffering? We must awaken to the fact that life is, and will remain, continuous suffering. It is by realizing that truth and thinking about it that I have been able to recover from my own periods of depression and the withering of my spirit.

What has changed over the ages is that the human race has become a parasite on the Earth and on nature. Our numbers have increased dramatically; we have become a destructive force on the planet. The power of this force means that we no longer fear the powers of nature or the supernatural, but, with the advance of science, have come to think of ourselves as the rulers of the entire universe.

There are those who cultivate a positive attitude toward life. Motivating yourself with positive thinking, trusting in human nature, holding out hope for the world's improvement, and living a life based on humanism and love is fine for those to whom this outlook comes naturally. To do so, however, sometimes means to leave much unseen and unfelt. To view the present state of human existence itself as cursed, and to base our lives on that belief, will strike many as absurd and warped. Who is this doomsayer? Who is this Cassandra? Those who see life through a dark glass can be as blind as those with rose-tinted spectacles.

There is the question, then, of holding ourselves in tension between these two extremes. We begin in darkness but must not let that darkness overwhelm us. We must keep the doors unlocked. If in that pitch-black darkness a single ray of light should be let in, if in this desert of our existence we might feel the touch of a warm breeze on our skin, it is a wonderful experience. I would like to think of it as a miraculous stroke of good fortune.

I believe it is necessary for us to completely overturn our view of life and begin from the recognition that life is a process of uninterrupted suffering. Just as one lives more vigorously after contemplating the closeness of death, cultivating a bleak view of human existence will bring one closest to rapture at the wonder life has to offer.

I call this negative thinking.

The Buddha As the Ultimate Negative Thinker

In daily life, I am sometimes treated rudely by those who have no regard for me as a human being. There are times when I think, "What awful people!" and I feel my gorge rising in anger. Several years ago, when I was visiting the Soviet Union, I encountered hostility several times a day. Many people, not only bureaucrats and officials but ordinary men and women on the street, took every opportunity to make an unpleasant show of the power, however small, they held over others. But then, suddenly, I would meet someone (often a person living on the edges of the society) who displayed an astonishingly honest and direct humanity and who overflowed with spontaneous, unaffected kindness. There is no way to describe the joy I felt at those encounters.

In Japanese there is an expression, "Rain of compassion from the dry heavens." Precisely because the earth is so parched and cracked, a single drop of rain can be precious. In the utter blackness, the light of a single lamp enlightens the dark soul.

As King Lear says in Shakespeare's tragedy, "When we are born, we cry that we are come / To this great stage of fools."* I have repeated this sentiment over and over in my writings. In this coliseum of wild beasts, where strong devour weak, on this spherical stage that is our world, where we act out a ridiculous comedy of errors, we appear—not of our own will, but set here without choice or say in the matter. King Lear, wandering the heath in the midst of the storm, knows that the infant's birth cry is the heart's cry of every human being, terribly frightened and anxious and utterly alone.

---

*_King Lear,_ Act IV, sc. vi, ls. 185–86.

Some may deride this view as negative and pessimistic, but this was the starting point for the Buddha. Emerging from a life of privilege and shelter, he looked directly at the reality of human existence and saw birth, old age, sickness, and death as its essence. This view of human existence as defined by birth, old age, sickness, and death is the ultimate expression of negative thinking.

The real question, then, is: What comes next? What follows from this insight? We are born in tears, we are weighed down by the heavy shackles of birth, old age, sickness, and death; is there any way for a person, as an individual, to live a life that is richly rewarding and filled with hope and vitality in spite of this burden? Or is it impossible? The twenty-nine-year-old Prince Gautama (later the Buddha) set out on a journey on which he would throw his entire being into solving this insoluble question. He abandoned his wife and child, abandoned a life of rank, fame, and ease, to embark on a quest for the key to the true nature of human existence.

Today we, too, should take a radically negative position as our starting point. Life is a series of hurts. The human race is a perpetrator of evil that harms the Earth, nature, and itself. Each of us suffers, grows old against his will, falls ill, and dies. We are born weeping, and we all die alone.

Let us accept this view of existence. And then let us ask: Although we may be born crying, is there not some way that we can die laughing? Is this not the true end and goal of every life?

I think this is extremely difficult, but the Buddha, who began from a radically negative point of view, may have achieved it. He died from illness, it is true, but he died with a smile on his face. The account of his death has him passing away after looking up at the twin sala trees that shaded him on his deathbed and saying, "The world is wonderful." Here was a man who started from the most radically negative viewpoint and arrived at the most radically affirmative stance before leaving this world. It was this achievement of the Buddha that has perplexed and inspired interest in his life and teachings even today, some two thousand years after his passing. It is an achievement that anyone, no matter how relentless their suffering, no matter how dark their experience of human nature, can capture.

A Boy on the Banks of the Taedong River

During the summer of my first year of junior high school, Japan was defeated in World War II. I was living in Pyongyang, in what is now North Korea. Our school was closed suddenly, and my days were filled with a combination of unimaginable freedom and chaos. One day, when the waters of the Taedong River were high from heavy rains, I decided to try to swim across the river. It was a very wide river.

The Taedong was a strange river. Its current sometimes reversed, often when the sea at its mouth at Chinnampo reached high tide. The river's upper layers of water and its undercurrent interacted in complex ways. I wasn't at all sure I could swim across it, but at thirteen I was unable to resist the temptation of a reckless adventure.

When I reached about the halfway point, I was suddenly overcome with an unexpected and bottomless terror. The water temperature and current suddenly changed. My arms and legs grew stiff and I was in danger of being pulled down by the undertow. I panicked and turned back toward the shore. Exhausted, I crawled up onto the shore and spent the rest of the day staring at the muddy yellow water swirling in whirlpools. As I watched, I had the strange feeling that my body and mind had been absorbed in that great flow and were being carried along with it to its final destination.

I think that was the first time that I became aware, however vaguely, of the huge, invisible current that we might call the power of fate.

From time to time, I can still recall the strange perception I experienced that day. It was a curious feeling, as if my own being was moving in some great invisible rhythm, and extended infinitely.

Since then I have seen many rivers; the Yabegawa and the Chikugogawa in my hometown, the Ongagawa in Chikuho, and many other rivers of Kyushu. As I travel around the world for my work, I have gazed at many rivers.

I have watched the flowing water of rivers in India, in Russia, in China and Latin America, never bored by their moving currents. In Soviet-occupied Prague, I stood on the Charles Bridge, gazing at the black waters of the Vltava River for hours. Whenever I stand on a riverbank I experience that feeling I had as a boy on the banks of the Taedong.

When I am in that still and timeless state, the same phrase beats in my mind like a spell. It is a very ordinary phrase:

A single drop of water in a mighty river.
A person is a single drop of water in a mighty river.

It is no more than a single small drop of water, but it is a part of the great flow, a part of the rhythm moving to the beat of eternity. This is the awareness that rises spontaneously within me as I watch a river flow.

Confucius, the great Chinese sage, and the twelfth-century Japanese poet Kamo no Chomei, among others, have used the metaphor of a river's flow to communicate many different thoughts and feelings. I can offer no organized presentation of my thoughts, as my illustrious predecessors have done, but I do have a strong and immediate feeling, a deep belief within my being like the throbbing of a pulse.

When our voyage as a single drop of water comes to its end, we return to the sea. Embraced by the Mother Sea, we are one with all the other drops, until the light and the warmth of the sun embraces us and carries us into the sky. And then we fall to earth again.

It is a childlike metaphor, I know; yet, I feel as if I can actually see it.

II. A Single Drop of Water in a Mighty River

A Drop in the River

To imagine an invisible, supernatural realm is to unconsciously come into contact with the very root of religious feeling. Although we may not always be aware of it, we live in surprisingly close contact with the realms of the spirit. When we feel an indescribable emotion watching a beautiful sunset, or feel a deep forest is eerie and frightening, or are moved by the sight of a weed pushing up through a crack in the asphalt, we are coming into contact with an invisible world.

I do not call such feelings animism and relegate them to the level of primitive, premodern thought. Nor do I like those who sneer at the ancient Japanese custom of worshipping gods and Buddhist deities together, even identifying them with each other, as the ignorant superstition of the masses. Religions do not originate in doctrines and organizations. They arise from natural human emotions.

Just as the experience of the transcendent brings one close to religious feeling, so does its opposite, the experience of utter horror.

When a person imagines hell and feels that "this world is hell," he has already taken a first step into the realm of religion. Not long after my epiphany on the Taedong River, I, along with many thousands of war refugees the world over, had my first experience of hell.

After the war there was a popular political poster with the slogan "Let us never again see the faces of starving children." When I saw it, I said to myself that it was the faces of starving adults that I never wanted to see again. When World War II ended I was in northern Korea, which was then part of the Japanese empire. The period that I spent as a refugee under the military rule of the Soviet Union has left me with several indelible memories that remain incredibly vivid to this day.

Under the extreme conditions of defeat and retreat, we children looked at adults as terrifying creatures. Although Korean and Soviet soldiers sometimes took pity on children and gave us rice cakes, black bread, or potatoes, often an adult would overpower us and steal our food. At that time we all learned a hard lesson, and we learned it in our very bones: There is nothing as frightening as a hungry adult.

There were also frequent cases of betrayal, of lynching, of rape, of selling children into slavery and prostitution. But what we experienced was nothing compared to the fate of those Japanese in areas nearer the Soviet border.

One of my friends, who was in a camp in Siberia, related the following story to me. "On winter nights," he said, "when you suddenly felt a horde of fleas attack you, you were happy. That meant the person lying next to you had died and whenever someone died, the two people sleeping on either side had the right to divide up his belongings, his socks and gloves and underwear." You'd welcome the fleas, thinking that tomorrow you could have the dead man's clothes.

My friend was marked by this experience, as I was by mine; we were both given brutal insights into this fable we call humanity. This is not merely a tale of extreme human suffering, of a civilized world turned upside down in the wake of massive violence, however. This is a story that is meant to awaken you to the darkness lying in wait, sometimes within the depths of your own soul. It is most likely true that you have never spent time in a Siberian prison waiting for the person next to you to die so that you might take his clothes. Most likely your life will be spared such misery. Nevertheless, you cannot congratulate yourself on the luck of living in a more enlightened time and place where such things could never happen.

Truly enlightened thinking is not about being lucky, or privileged, or content with one's lot in life. Truly enlightened thinking only takes place when we have stared into the bottomless possibilities of human suffering and discovered light. The only way to reach that point is to descend to the ultimate limit of negative thinking. Hell is not something preserved for Russian jailers, or adults who steal food from children. Hell is where we live now, hell is the prison of suffering that defines our existence. We are not born to the ringing of bells, in a dream paradise of singing birds and blossoming flowers and the complacency of the middle class; we are born in hell.

But in this hell, we sometimes encounter unexpected small joys, friendship, the kind acts of strangers, and the miracle of love. We experience moments when we are filled with courage, when the world sparkles with hopes and dreams. There are even times when we are deeply grateful to have been born a human being. There are times when we laugh heartily with others.

Those moments are paradise. Paradise is not another realm; it is not something preserved for those who have been given the opportunity to do good in the world. It is here, here in the very midst of the hell of this world.

Once one has accepted that hell is the inescapable present, one will experience an astonishing joy. Some may come to see their self, which until then had been rushing about in suffering and distress, as comical, even childish.

I believe that I have been able to pull myself back from suicide and pick up the pieces and start again because I was able to tell myself that this world is originally and essentially senseless, cruel, and filled with suffering and tragedy.

But the early realization that this world is hell is not the only thing that saved me, in later years, from suicide. I also had clear memories that, unbelievably, even under those cruel and extreme circumstances, there was human kindness, there was honesty, there were consideration, caring, and at times laughter, happiness, free-dom, and deep feelings. Even among adults, there were those who kept their promises, those who shared their food. When I encoun-tered one of these people, I felt as if I had met a Buddha.

Yes, paradise does exist here within hell.

Living Without Expectations

Today we sit in an Italian restaurant and criticize the quality of the olive oil in which we dip our bread, or we complain about the heat in the commuter train being too high. We've progressed far beyond worrying about fleas and hunger and, in that progress, our delusions have multiplied. We believe we can conquer suffering, illness, and even death.

Yet, how can we forget that we are born into this life crying? That when we die, we die alone. Although our lover, our family, our dear friends, may be with us on our deathbeds, they cannot die with us. We have support and companionship in life, but in death we are on our own. Indeed, we are born into this world with illness already inside us. Buddhism teaches that human beings carry 404 illnesses. We may eventually conquer such diseases as cancer and AIDS, but we will never conquer death itself. Our lives are a journey, a daily walk, step by step, toward death. Life itself is not only a progress, day after day, toward death, but we are also carriers of death, and there will never be a method to suppress its eventual manifestation.

We part from all we meet. No matter how dearly a husband and wife love each other, one of them will precede the other in death, and they will be forced to part. Their harmonious life together stops on that day. Our parents will die. If we are very lucky, we will die before our children, but even this is not guaranteed.

No matter how surrounded by love and affection we may seem to be, we must take responsibility for ourselves as we face death.

That is why parents must not expect anything from their children. Children should not expect anything from their parents. Although you love someone, you should not expect to be loved in return. Aren't love, kindness, and the works of Good Samaritans actually completely selfless acts? When you have realized selflessness, a new awareness is born in you.

When you no longer have any expectations, the unexpected kindness of strangers and small acts of consideration become like "sweet manna from heaven." The feeling that rises spontaneously within one's heart at such times is true gratitude. When one is accustomed to kindness, one naturally loses the feeling of gratitude. That's why it's so important not to become accustomed to it. One must constantly return oneself to the spiritual starting point of no expectations.

Husbands should not expect anything from their wives, or wives from their husbands. Both love and family ties undergo aging, sickness, and death. It is a mistake to expect that these bonds will naturally go on forever.

Although a person may serve his country, he should expect nothing from the nation or the government. Of course no one should expect anything from a bank, a business, or an employer. Nor should one entrust one's soul to a temple or a church. One must not look to a thinker or a philosopher to be a guide to life.

Students shouldn't expect anything of their teachers, nor should teachers from students. Yet, if, by chance, there is a moment in the classroom in which the teacher and the students feel linked in the common endeavor of learning, it is a wonderful thing. We should be as moved by and grateful for such moments as if they were miracles. They are miracles, and we should engrave this rare knowledge deeply in our consciousness and memory.

Although written records may disappear, memory remains. Such memories are sure to play an important role when, once again, we find our spirits withering.

Our lives are nothing more than a single drop in the flow of a mighty river. Together with an infinite number of other drops, we form that river, and we flow steadily and surely to the sea. At times we leap, we sing; at times we move silently on toward the sea. We have reached the time to look back over the last fifty years, which we spent desperately pursuing a dream of scaling the peaks, and reflect on the truth that we are flowing gently to the sea, from where we will return to the skies.

Our only choice, I believe, is to start over from that realization.

My Father

My father was born into a farming family in a mountain village on the border between Fukuoka Prefecture and Kumamoto Prefecture. It was very deep in the mountains, and they got their drinking water from little mountain streams. Of course there was no electricity. Although they were farmers, they were so poor that they had their own rice-ration book. His family grew tea. The heavy mountain mists made for delicious tea leaves. They also grew tangerines. They harvested bamboo shoots. From sumac trees, they made wax for candles. They also harvested the bark of mulberry and other trees, which was the raw material for making Japanese paper and banknotes. They collected wild plants such as *konnyaku* and *kuzu* that were made into foodstuffs. They did a little of everything, as all farmers did in those days, and in spite of it they were poor.

In such families, only the eldest son could inherit. Customarily, and this was true of my father, the second and third sons had to leave the village and find some other work. What ways were there for a young man born in that period, a time when enterprise and self-reliance were so strongly encouraged, to escape his mountain village and make a place for himself in the world?

My father entered a teachers school in Kokura. At that time both Kokura and Yahata were big cities with long histories; now they have been merged into a single city, Kitakyushu. My father no doubt worked hard and got good grades. He was probably a work-study student, and along with his studies he put a lot of energy into sports such as kendo and gymnastics, working hard to master both the civil and martial arts of a classical education. He had already reached the third rank in kendo while a student, which indicates that he must have been a very hard worker.

After graduating, he found a job teaching elementary school in the countryside in Kyushu, and a new life started for him. As a young teacher in his twenties he was transferred from school to school in Fukuoka Prefecture, not far from the area in which he had been born.

At one of those schools, he met my mother, who was also a teacher. She had graduated from the Fukuoka Women's Teachers College and was also an elementary school teacher. I don't know much about their courtship but I know they fell in love, married, and I was born.

In the photographs of my mother from back then, she seems to be a modern woman. In one she is wearing a hat with a frill and holding a tennis racket.

It seems my father was an ambitious young man who worked hard to advance himself. Later he left Fukuoka and took a teaching post in Korea, which was a Japanese colony at the time.

The people who went to Japan's overseas colonies were usually ambitious, active people who felt frustrated or held back on the Japanese mainland and wanted to blaze new trails for themselves. No doubt my father thought that if he stayed in Japan he would amount to nothing more than the head teacher of some small, rural elementary school. Dissatisfied with that prospect, he decided to try his luck in the colonies—in his case, Korea—and start a new life.

One of the memories of my father that has stayed with me through the years is the sight I would catch of him, when I woke up at 3:00 A.M. to use the toilet, sitting in a little room near the entrance to our house, wrapped in a heavily padded coat, reading and taking notes by lamplight.

My mother would be awake, too, and would occasionally bring him tea or something to eat.

In the first town we lived in in Korea, there were only two Japanese families, ours and that of a police officer. Everyone else was Korean. My father's first job was as the principal of a school attended entirely by Korean students.

It was hard work for a young man in his twenties, and photographs show him with a little mustache, like Hitler's—no doubt an attempt, though somewhat strained, to look older and give him some authority.

He continued to take examinations for promotions, making a terrific effort to raise himself up in the educational profession.

In the winter nights, we could hear the far-off howling of wild dogs or wolves. Then the night would fall silent again, interrupted occasionally by a sharp, cracking sound, like ice breaking. When I think of my father sitting up through those cold winter nights, studying hard and taking notes under the light of the lamp, I feel a pang in my heart, I admit.

My mother hated the trailing howl of those wild dogs. I'm sure it frightened her. The local people called them *nukte*. "Ah, the *nukte* are howling again," I remember her saying, and then softly adding that she wished we could move to a larger town soon.

And so it was that my father passed his early years in struggle and hard work.

Then one day many telegrams of congratulation arrived at our house. After passing all of those examinations, one after another, my father was transferred to an elementary school in a slightly bigger town, then again to a slightly bigger town, until, just before the time when I was to enter elementary school, he was appointed to a teaching post at Nandaimon Elementary school in Seoul, a very prestigious school. At last his dream of living in a big city was realized.

My father's untiring efforts to raise himself up in the world were slowly paying off. His next position was as a teacher at a secondary school teachers college in Pyongyang. This occurred about the time I was a third grader.

My father was really overjoyed at this new appointment. At last he was in secondary education, and he felt that a bright future awaited him. He was more than halfway to the top.

Apart from the Taedong River that ran through Pyongyang, there was also a lovely mountain called Peony Peak. The teachers college in Pyongyang was no doubt a very fine institution, given the importance of the city. We lived in the faculty housing and my father's job was to train the next generation of teachers there.

He was also a member of the Martial Arts Association, and while at this school he consolidated his standing in the educational profession. It was, I think, a very good time for him.

It was during this period that he used to wake me up early every morning and make me practice kendo and swordsmanship for about thirty minutes in the school courtyard. I just hated it. After that he would sit me down in the living room and force me to memorize long, difficult passages from such ancient works as *Nihon Shoki* (The chronicles of Japan).

Fragments of some of that mumbo jumbo are still left in my head; he used to make me sight-read these texts without understanding them. My father loved reciting Chinese poetry, and at night he would sing Chinese-style poetry for which he had composed melodies. Even today Chinese-style poetry is chanted as an accompaniment for sword dances. He would chant his Chinese-style poetry almost every night.

To tell the truth, I thought he was a little gloomy. And as Japan was reaching for the heights, trying to become a rich nation with a strong military, I think he was a patriot and proud of it.

His area of specialty was Japanese and Chinese, and so our bookshelves were filled with works of Norinaga Motoori, Atsutane Hirata, and Kitaro Nishida. But at night, he would flop down on his bed, in summer just wearing his underpants, and let out a huge sigh. It was such a contrast from his usual proud demeanor as a teacher, a kendo master—this huge, almost helpless sigh.

Whereas before he had often studied all through the night, from the time we moved to Pyongyang he started to have a drink at night and then go to sleep early. As a child, I always wondered what that great sigh meant.

In addition to his sigh, I remember that he always burned moxa on his scrawny right leg, at a place just a little below the knee and to the right. He had a dark scar there from moxibustion. Every night he'd burn the moxa there, sigh, and go to sleep. Lately, I frequently find my mind returning to that memory of my father.

The truth is that I feel much closer to that father, the one who would stretch his arms and legs out and sigh from the depths of his heart, the father who would burn moxa on his leg and then fall asleep, than I do to the militarist, the imperialist, father. When I remember him these days, I feel a strange intimacy with him that I never had in life.

In 1945, when I was in my first year of junior high school, the unimaginable happened: Japan was defeated, and the life of my family was transformed.

For some reason, although I have a vague memory of the day we learned of the defeat, I have no clear or concrete recollections. It is as if they were hidden behind a veil of mist.

The ambitions of my father, whose self-esteem depended so heavily on his post at the teachers college, and who hoped to rise even further, were crushed by this turn of events; they fell to the ground with a clatter.

But I think the destruction of our family life was a greater shock to him.

Soviet troops soon entered Pyongyang, and the city was in chaos.

Our home was taken over by the Soviets, and we Japanese fled in a group, carrying little more than the clothes on our backs. We were relocated to a large warehouse-type structure and there lived the lives of refugees. My mother died on September 19, a month after the war's end. This was a perhaps the pivotal event in my father's life.

All of my father's past accomplishments, all of his hopes and plans, had been destroyed in a flash. This would have been enough to bring him to his knees, but then, at the same time, he lost the love of his life, his companion of so many years, his one true support.

Facing such enormous disillusionment in both his public and private lives, his entire persona—the imperialist, the kendo master, the nationalist, the teacher—crumbled under its own weight, and he became a pitiful figure, drinking from morning to night.

As I said, I was a first-year junior high school student, and after the defeat it was easier for children to find work—for example, as a houseboy in a Russian officer's home—than it was for adults. My father began a useless existence, and I was half disgusted with him as I busily went about finding the means to feed my little brother and sister. Every day I went into town, thinking of myself as the little master of our household. That was how I spent the days immediately after the defeat.

The truth is that I also felt a need to protect my father. Here was the man who had forced me to practice kendo and to recite passages from ancient texts, the man who had sung difficult Chinese poems, the man toward whom I felt not only respect but a kind of distance. Now he was useless, drunk from morning to night, humming old popular tunes with half-closed eyes, a man utterly transformed.

It may have been a little arrogant for a thirteen-year-old boy to be thinking such things, but I did feel a strong duty to support and help my father, the beginning of a very strong, personal feeling for this man now that our roles were, in a way, reversed.

Eventually, after an extended period of life as refugees, we succeeded in escaping to the city of Kaesong across the border into South Korea. At that time Kaesong was under the control of United States forces, and we thought that if we could get that far, we could somehow get repatriated to Japan.

After living for a while in a refugee camp in Kaesong, we were given passage on a U.S. military transport ship, the Liberty, and arrived at Hakata in Kyushu.

Here my father's wanderings, and mine as well, at last came to an end. And here, too, the third period of my father's life, his final years in postwar Japan, began.

Life in Japan

When I look back on the life my father lived after returning to Japan, I am pained; at the same time, it seems to represent something larger than just my own family's fate: some larger human destiny affecting an entire generation.

My father was unable to stop drinking even after returning to Japan, and he went from one job to another. He was a tangerine wholesaler, a tea salesman, a dealer in stolen goods on the black market, and a bootlegger, making liquor from sweet potatoes. He once ran a sort of drive-in along the road crossing from Kumamoto Prefecture to Fukuoka Prefecture. Anyway, he tried his hand at many different things, and the time passed.

At the end, he returned to teaching for a short time, but soon after he fell ill and died.

When I look back at my father's life following the war, I confess I cannot detect the slightest trace of the bright young man burning with ambition that I had known before. Instead, he spent his days in the kind of loose and undisciplined living that is often associated with "bohemian" writers and artists. He once collapsed, coughing up blood, at a racetrack.

I helped my father in his many occupations, and at the same time was always thinking of a way to get away to Tokyo, where I could build a new and entirely different life of my own.

At times I believed I had learned nothing of any use from my father. He made me memorize passages from the classics, learn by rote many Chinese-style poems, and achieve a certain proficiency in kendo, but these skills I regarded as negative contributions to my life. My father often lectured me about many things, but I don't remember any of them. Recently, however, I have come to think that I received a great deal from him.

For example, that huge sigh that he always let out when he collapsed on his bed. When lately I notice myself heaving that same big sigh, I realize that while it is just the human action of a sigh, I feel it is also an expression of the very essence of the human condition.

Here he was, a representative of the ruling empire sent out to one of its colonies, falling into his bed and letting out a great sigh. I often think that within that sigh rests some great weight, a weight shared by all of us that is a part of being alive.

My father, sighing. Not the father of the grand words, the father who sighs deeply. The father who, upon returning to Japan, ruined his health by drinking. And the father who was brought down by illness in his mid-fifties and died. Whenever I think of that father, I see a more human aspect, something essential to his life, to our lives.

Joy is important, but so is sadness. It is important to have hope, but also to despair. It is important to be strong and confident, but also to sigh deeply.

I have inherited my father's sigh. It is his gift to me, whenever I think and feel.

Heading Down the Hill

Now that I am in my late sixties, I have come to feel that human existence has a kind of indescribable sadness or pity to it.

There are times in life when we climb to the heights, aiming for the peak. There are also times when, after crossing the peak, we head slowly back down to the valley, our shoulders hunched against the cold autumn wind at our backs. But whichever direction we are heading in, it is human nature to sigh. All people, all around the world and at all times, live a life of sighs.

Being able to appreciate the weight of that sigh handed down from father to son is actually very important in living a better life. It is, I think, the foundation that allows us to live our lives with courage.

In that sense, although I may have learned nothing from my father the educator, although I may have no interest in the classical authors he so fondly read, I am sustained by him, because he has given me his sigh.

And I also recall my mother's face as she looked at my father; although supporting him in everything, revealed in some corner of her expression was the gaze of someone watching a weak, pitiful figure. I can recall her watching him vigorously wielding his sword in kendo, his shoulders square and taut, with an expression that seemed to say, "You don't have to prove anything to me."

My mother died at forty-two and my father in his mid-fifties. The early deaths of both my parents impressed upon me the fact that we all die; our lives are not very long, and they are filled with disappointment, despair, and disillusion.

I can think of no actual words of my parents that have sustained me over the years, but their early deaths awakened me to the presence of death in life, to the fate of all human beings, and for that I am, I think, very fortunate.

I have read many books. I have sampled difficult philosophies. I have engaged the great thinkers of the past. But I have gained more from my father's sigh, his wasted later years, and my mother's unexpected death, than from any of these.

We Humans Are Very Insignificant Beings

Once, when I was looking at the paintings of the Sistine Chapel in the Vatican, I had a strange experience. I was overwhelmed by the huge, muscular depiction of Christ in Michelangelo's great masterpiece The Last Judgment. The painting seemed to trumpet the central insight of the Renaissance: the greatness of humankind. Until then, the human race had been regarded as petty and insignificant in comparison to the glory and might of God and the power and authority of His Church. I had always preferred the pre-Renaissance painting style, with its more stylized, two-dimensional portraits. I felt a strong attraction to the slightly stooped, gaunt depictions of Christ and other figures with their ribs protruding. Now I understood why. Yet, even the arrogance of the Renaissance pales beside our notions of ourselves today. Now we consider ourselves the most important form of life in the universe.

I think that we humans need to rediscover humility. We cannot go on forever singing the Renaissance paean to the glory of humankind. Isn't it time that we saw ourselves as the small and helpless beings we are, and lived our lives more humbly, our eyes lowered in self-abnegation? I would like us to imagine ourselves once again as insignificant, a trifling form of existence. But the life of the universe resides in each thing, no matter how small, down to a single dewdrop on the leaf of a plant. If "life of the universe" seems too grand a phrase, perhaps we can say the "breath of the universe."

Rain falls from the skies, rushes over the leaves of the plants and trees, and a single drop falls to the forest floor, where it is absorbed. Underground water currents surface and form small rivulets. These join in streams that in turn join into rivers, which run over the plains and eventually flow into the world's mighty oceans.

Our individual lives are like drops of water in those mighty rivers flowing to the sea. The sea accepts all the waters of the world, clear or cloudy, pure or polluted, without discrimination. Eventually the warmth of the sun causes the water of the oceans to evaporate and form clouds in the sky, from which once again rain falls down to the earth, and the journey from land to sea begins again.

This is how I imagine the story of life. It is a very ordinary, even simplistic story, but recently I have come to take it quite seriously.

Isn't it by inventing stories and believing in them that we humans are finally able to transcend the bonds of birth, old age, sickness, and death?

Those who feel they have no alternative to suicide must invent such a story. Just as there are times when one tries to die but fails, there are times when even the best effort to live does not succeed. But when I envision myself as a single drop of water in a great river, I find that I no longer feel the need to bring my life to an end by my own doing.

"The Good Die Young"

The Japanese word *jokuse* (defiled or polluted world) was originally a Buddhist term, used to describe the defilement and turmoil of human existence.

A person's view of the age in which he is living depends upon his place in it. When I think about politics, business, the medical establishment, and education today, I am so disgusted with what's going on that I don't even have energy to protest. I won't give specific examples. Even writing this much depresses me terribly.

Yet, I have never raised my voice loudly to protest any of these things, and I have almost never written strong social criticism. The most I do is grumble quietly to myself or drop an occasional sarcastic comment. This may well be because I have a guilty suspicion tucked away in some corner of my soul that I am little more than a minnow swimming in the dirty waters of that defiled world. I am no longer young. I know that I am one of the bad guys, who has in his life up to now pushed aside many other people in my own rush to survive and to get ahead.

This is by no means false humility. I have deep in my heart a feeling like a heavy stone, which makes me see myself as a worthless person, beyond all salvation.

When I was a boy, on the evening of the day that the Japanese defeat was announced, several of my father's Korean students came to our home. They were wearing red armbands, and a few of them were carrying guns at the waist. The words "People's Committee" were dyed on the armbands.

They told us that we should get on a train as soon as possible. "Trains are still leaving from Heijo Station. Most of the families of the military officers and officials have packed their things and are moving south."

My father, perhaps feeling threatened by his students' newly assertive attitude, merely nodded silently.

My mother, who was ill and spent much of her time in bed, anxiously asked my father, "What should we do? Should we pack our things right now?" But he shook his head. "Japan is in a terrible state right now. Let's wait awhile to see what happens." Then he went into his study and began burning his notebooks in the yard. They were the rough draft of a book that he had been working on for years.

The radio kept saying, "Public security will be preserved. Japanese citizens should refrain from rash actions and remain where they are." "Listen to what the radio is saying," said my father, and, based on what he heard, he rejected my mother's suggestion that we leave. He always absolutely obeyed whatever instructions he heard on the radio.

So my family did not go to Heijo Station, on that day or afterward. In less than a month our home and all our possessions had been confiscated by the Soviet army, and we were forced to place my sick mother in a cart and wander through the streets of the city. Our lives as refugees, without passports, continued for over a year. My mother died. Finally, carrying a lock of my dead mother's hair, I fled with my siblings south, over the 38th parallel, and was taken into a U.S.-run refugee camp in South Korea, from where I was shipped home to Japan.

One must not blindly trust one's country, and one must not blindly trust oneself, either.

I managed to survive that period of indescribable chaos, and to live to this day. Whenever I remember the time, I instinctively lower my eyes and drop my voice. Although I have written many books, I have written very little about what I saw and experienced then. I doubt I ever will.

What was it that made the difference between those who survived and those who never returned, but fell by the wayside? Did those with strong faith survive? Or those with physical strength or intelligence? Was it those who didn't lose hope, who retained a positive attitude?

I have something buried deep in my heart, a voice I can always hear coming from somewhere inside me saying, "No, that's not it. The bad people survived, and the good people all died.

"You haven't forgotten that, have you?" asks the voice.

It was the ones with the stronger egos, the ones willing to push others aside, the ones who possessed a powerful, self-centered will to live, who survived under those extreme conditions. It was those who were twice as selfish as others, steeped in bad karma, who made it through.

I was thirteen. Carrying my little sister on my back and pulling my little brother along by the hand, I ran to the 38th parallel. If my brother was too weak to keep up with me, I was fully prepared to leave him where he fell and keep on running. The unthinking life force of my instinct for self-preservation pushed my malnourished body forward.

My brother died of cancer in his mid-forties. He did not like conflict with others and he always treated me with respect; even as a boy, he was preternaturally mature. By his teens he seemed resigned to his lot, and he was remarkably gentle in spirit. When I became recognized as a new writer in my early thirties, it almost seemed as if it was his wish to follow in my footsteps.

I remember almost painfully his favorite phrase: "*Ii ja nai?*" It's difficult to translate its exact nuances into English, but perhaps "What's the use in getting so worked up?" is close. He would half-whisper it, in his Kyushu accent. It was his response to my outbursts about things that were happening in my work or in the world, spoken when I would strike out in anger and excitement at those around me. He'd let me say all I had to say and then, with an ironic smile, drop his soft "What's the use in getting so worked up?" almost as if he were speaking to himself.

When he died suddenly, the pop lyric "Only the good die young" came to me. I can't help but think that those who survive in our world are the sinners, whose very existence depends upon the death of the good.

Qu Yuan's Anger and the Fisherman's Song

I heard this story long ago.

In ancient China there was a man named Qu Yuan (circa 340–278 B.C.). He lived during the Warring States period, which was from 403 B.C. to 221 B.C. In this period of instability and conflict, he lamented the state that his kingdom and his people had fallen into and he did his best to serve them well. For all his efforts, he nonetheless was slandered by rivals and condemned to exile, forced to live a wandering life in desolate regions. It is thought that Qu Yuan's superior abilities, his unwavering sense of right and wrong, and his determination to live a life of the utmost integrity aroused the resentment of others.

Tired of spending long years in exile and despondent because of his frustrated aspirations, Qu Yuan arrived, lamenting loudly, at the banks of the broad Canglang River. As he stood there looking up at the heavens and spewing out his angry denunciation of this corrupt and defiled world, a fisherman approached in his boat. The fisherman remarked that Qu Yuan appeared to be a man of high rank, and asked what was the matter.

Qu Yuan replied that everyone in the world was dishonest, and that the world itself was utterly corrupt. In such a world, he and he alone had lived a pure and honest life. Everyone else was as if completely drunk on wine, and he alone was sober. That is why, he said, he had been driven from office and was condemned to spend his life in helpless frustration.

The fisherman listened to Qu Yuan, nodding, and then asked: "What you say may well be true, but have you ever thought of any other way of living, an alternative to holding yourself above this defiled, corrupt world?"

Qu Yuan answered that he would rather throw himself into the river and become food for the fishes than to stain his perfect integrity by accepting the corruption of the world. That, he said, was his chosen way of life, it was who he was.

The fisherman smiled softly and, beating time against the side of his boat, began to sing a song. These were the words:

When the waters of the Canglang are pure
Use them to wash the cords of your cap.
When the waters of the Canglang are muddy
Use them to wash your feet.

The fisherman then sailed away into the distance, never looking back.

The story of Qu Yuan and the fisherman is very popular in China, appearing in many forms. People like Qu Yuan are not rare today. There are talented people with high ideals who try to live their lives with complete integrity. Our polluted world must be very hard for them to bear. Clearly, Qu Yuan was a fine man. But the impudent song of the fisherman also contains an important truth for those of us who live in this world.

The water of the mighty river is sometimes clean and pure, sometimes muddy. In fact, it may most often be muddy. What use is it to spend your life angrily denouncing or lamenting this fact? Isn't it better to do something, small as it may be? That's what I think, as I sit rubbing my own dirty feet.

When the Water Is Muddy, Wash Your Feet

How, in terms of Qu Yuan's story, would we describe our present age?

It seems to me that these last several years have been marked by an unprecedented flood of swirling currents of polluted, muddy waters. The Canglang River is yellow with silt, obscuring the fish and river bottom completely.

The real workings of the realms of government and business have recently been stripped bare for all to see. We have seen how medicine and welfare services, which are supposed to be protecting our lives, have become big businesses that treat their human "clients" shoddily. We have been made keenly aware of the impotence of our schools and educational institutions, and felt the pain of not being able to comprehend the thoughts or actions of our children. We think it useless to seek strong direction and guidance in life from religion or philosophy.

If I were a twenty-year-old, I am sure I would think that the world was full of lies. In fact, not just young people but those who are the core of today's society, working hard to get by in it, feel the same way.

Qu Yuan may have lived in ancient times, but we today feel his outrage and despair as if it were our own.

"The world is idiotic, it's true, but I can't entirely sympathize with Qu Yuan. While I don't have the courage to live a completely corrupt life, yet, if that is the way of the world, I can't very well oppose it all by myself. I suppose I'll just have to not think about it too deeply and try to get along as best I can."

Isn't this how most people deal with the problem? In reality we are an undependable lot, unable to be completely good or evil.

I detect the wisdom and determination of the hardy common people in the words of the fisherman to Qu Yuan.

When you have the good fortune to find a clear river, you wash your precious belongings. You can wash your soul; you can wash your face. When the water is a muddy yellow, there's still no reason to stand there at the bank filled with anger or sadness. Look down at your feet. Look! You've been walking through the mud and now your feet are plastered with it. Or maybe you think that every part of your body is absolutely clean and pure and sparkling?

Like the fish that live in the river, like the animals that live in the fields, people, too, are living in a world that is always changing, minute by minute. This, perhaps, is the message that the fisherman was trying convey with his song. At the same time, Qu Yuan had his own way of living. That, too, must be recognized. He had his own ideals, which he defended, and then he threw himself into the river and drowned. That, too, is a way to live. While quietly nodding in agreement at the fisherman's words, people have also long told the story of Qu Yuan out of sympathy for his firm integrity and commitment to his ideals.

Our big problem is deciding how to live in the kind of world we find ourselves in today. How do those who have experienced desperation interpret the story of Qu Yuan? Speaking for myself, although I sympathize with Qu Yuan, I sense something larger and more important in the song of the fisherman. Don't simply lament the dirty water. If the Canglang River is muddy, wash your feet in it. Whispering that phrase quietly to myself, I live.

Is There No Truth in the World?

Prince Shotoku (574–622) was a seminal figure in Japanese history, overseeing the introduction of Chinese culture and many new concepts and ideas, including Buddhism, to Japanese society. He had grand ideals, and with those ideals he was able to carry out several important changes in Japanese society. His time was the first period of reform in Japanese history. But Prince Shotoku died with a brief, riddle-like couplet on his lips.

It began, "The world is vain and empty." This was followed by a religious statement, "Only the Buddha is true." I find myself attracted to the first line of the couplet, "The world is vain and empty," because I find in it a very real human sentiment, a kind of existential sigh, of a different tenor than the more orthodox Buddhist sentiment expressed in the second line.

In Buddhism, the vain and empty stands in contrast to the true and meaningful; it refers to this phenomenal world we see around us. I can't help but feel that what Prince Shotoku really meant was "What an idiotic, worthless world this is!" I sense lurking in these words an unbearable scorn and disappointment. From ancient times to today, our world has always been this kind of place. From that feeling of resignation arises the second line of the couplet: "Only the Buddha is true."

My feeling, I confess, is that both vain emptiness and true meaning are to be found here in our world. There is a meaning to life, and there is meaninglessness. And although good people and evil people exist, I have no desire to divide them into two opposing camps. People, it seems to me, are volatile, dangerous beings who, depending upon their circumstances and their relationships with others, can be either good or evil. Our world is in a constant state of flux, change, and flow.

"You Can't Do What You Can't Do"

I am not a go-getter. I'm the opposite, actually. I am remarkably undisciplined.

But from long ago I have always wanted to be a go-getter. When I was in junior high school, I had a sign saying Work Hard! pasted up over my desk. That was about the extent of my effort, though: an empty gesture to hard work instead of the real thing. In high school, I changed the sign to Self-control.

But no matter how hard I spur myself on, by nature I just can't stick to anything for very long. Although I know there are things I must do and things that it would be to my tremendous advantage to do, I just can't get around to doing them. I'm careless in every aspect of my life, and not any good at finishing things up neatly.

I wonder what is behind this? I don't think it can be genetic.

Both my parents were accredited teachers and very serious and organized people.

It may be that the radical shift in values I experienced when I was young resulted in the disorderly fashion of my life today. Somewhere deep inside I have a strong feeling that no matter how much personal effort I make, I am almost powerless in the face of great social changes and historical upheavals.

Some things just don't work; some things just can't be done. When an individual's efforts and good intentions are not rewarded, they aren't rewarded. Deep in my heart I believe, in fact, that that is the way this world works most of the time.

I was shocked when in my teens I heard the expression, "Honesty doesn't pay." What? Did anyone ever really believe that honesty did pay? I was astonished that such an obvious truth would be worth repeating.

Although some might dismiss that as the twisted thinking of a sarcastic child, I cannot so easily dismiss that feeling, even today, so many years later.

There are extremely rare occasions in our world, however, when honesty does pay. That is a fact. I have witnessed several examples of this myself. And each time I was very deeply moved.

There are also occasions when hard work is rewarded. It happens very rarely, but it does happen. I do not think that effort is wasted. But the chances of effort being rewarded in our world are so rare that it would not be an exaggeration to call such cases miracles.

To speak plainly, honesty usually does not pay. And effort is hardly ever rewarded.

I concede that my point of view is warped. It is certainly not normal. There are ordinary times and extraordinary times. Each hill has an up and a down side. There are favorable and unfavorable winds.

The real question is, What kind of age are we living in now?

III. Honen, Shinran, and Rennyo

The Words of Three Men Who Have Been My Supports

Life is hard. No matter how fortunate one's situation may seem, life presents all sorts of difficulties. No one can escape them.

A person may be financially well off but have health problems. Or one may have good health but family problems and conflicts with relatives. There are also the more abstract difficulties we encounter in seeking love and trying to fulfill our personal aspirations. There are the difficulties of mental suffering and insecurity, and of frustrated desires.

There is of course the difficulty of money, of earning one's bread. Even a person who has none of these problems may have more difficulties of a "higher" level, such as feeling that life has no meaning, or that there is nothing in the world to rely on. There is also the pain of feeling that one doesn't truly exist.

Life is hard. It's only natural to sometimes feel that one can't go on living.

When I feel that way, the words and deeds of Honen

(1133–1212), Shinran (1173–1263), and Rennyo (1415–1499) are a great aid.

To put it simply, these three religious leaders give me the strength to live this difficult life, to go on without giving up.

I feel an aura surrounding these men that prevents me from falling into the pit of depression in this life of pain and anxiety, an aura that supports me in times of crisis and gives me a sense of well-being.

Honen is regarded as the founder of the Pure Land sect in Japan, but I do not pay much attention to sects. I look at Honen primarily as the teacher to whom Shinran entrusted himself and as the master who Shinran continued to revere all his life. Rennyo was a follower of Shinran, and he spent his life popularizing Shinran's teachings among the masses during a troubled time.

Hell Is Inevitable

In Japan, people will often refer to "the paradise of the Pure Land," leading to the belief that paradise and the Pure Land are one and the same, but I don't think this is the case.

The Pure Land is not paradise. Rather, paradise and hell—its opposite—refer to this world in which we pass our daily lives. In *Tannisho* (Lamenting heresies), Shinran uttered a famous phrase: "Hell is inevitable" (*jigoku wa ichijo*). Many read this as a statement that when we die we are all without exception bound for hell, but I do not choose to read it that way.

I read "inevitable," or *ichijo,* as "now," "the reality that is inevitably here before us." I am not afraid of going to hell after death because I have already been there. A self driven by desires, one that harms the planet and other people, tells lie after lie, and is deeply bound by all sorts of foolhardy attachments, is something we all have in common.

This foolish self that has so little chance of salvation, is so incapable of resisting burning desire and attachment; these undeniably real days and nights, lived under the constant torment of monstrous delusions: Such is hell.

With our anxieties about death and illness, our discriminating selves and the pain of being discriminated against, our rampant anger and envy, we are all residents of hell.

But according to Shinran, religion is a ray of light that illuminates hell. Religious faith exists to succor the suffering spirit. That is why all those who live in hell will eventually return to the Pure Land. In our daily lives, there are moments when we can believe this. That is paradise. But paradise almost never endures for long. In a moment the joy of paradise passes, and the jagged peaks of hell loom again.

Life is a constant passage back and forth between these two states of hell and paradise.

"Birth in the Pure Land" means accepting the great story of life. No matter what kind of life you have led, after death we all return as drops of water to the great river, and eventually rise to the heavens.

Where Do We Go After Death?

Who was Shinran and what did he teach?

Above all, Shinran was a man of deep humanity. Shinran founded a school of Buddhism unique to Japan. He was originally a follower of Honen, who taught the exclusive practice of the *nembutsu,* the recitation of the phrase "Namu Amida Butsu" ("I take refuge in Amida Buddha"). Amida was one of the names or avatars of the Buddha, from the Sanskrit name Amitabha.

I don't believe, however, that Shinran's faith in Amida Buddha was a kind of monotheistic faith, a belief in a single godlike figure, as many have argued. Although he may not have preached faith in the myriad Shinto gods of traditional Japanese belief, he did at least accept the many Buddhas and bodhisattvas of Mahayana Buddhism, and it was from among them that he selected Amida Buddha and advocated exclusive devotion to him. Actually, it seemed more as if the beneficent Amida Buddha had chosen him. Perhaps Amida Buddha had such particular and special qualities for the people of that age that he extended his hand to welcome followers.

Westerners are more familiar with Zen Buddhism than the Pure Land Buddhism that Shinran taught. Zen and Pure Land are probably the two main currents of Japanese Buddhism and they differ from each other in several ways. Zen has always been a relatively aristocratic tradition, attracting first the nobility and later the leaders of the warrior (samurai) class. It emphasizes hard effort to achieve enlightenment, either through meditation or deep introspection. Zen followers must leave the world and become monks, living together in monastic communities and following their rules. Pure Land Buddhism, in contrast, teaches a simple practice that anyone can do: the recitation of the Buddha's name. While Zen emphasizes the spiritual effort, Pure Land Buddhism emphasizes faith. Zen teaches that each person is a Buddha and must realize his or her enlightenment. Pure Land Buddhism teaches that Amida Buddha, who has already attained enlightenment, exists to save anyone who calls on his name with sincere faith. As a result,

Pure Land Buddhism has attracted a following among the common man.

Because of the importance of Amida Buddha in Pure Land Buddhism, many people seem to think that it is a religion that worships the Buddha as a god, and that Buddha is some type of visual representation of him—an image, a painting, something cast in the figure of a human being. But if we look at the true core of Shinran's teachings, the image of the Buddha is merely a means to assist faith.

Aside from the chosen few who are engaged in special religious practice or find faith after undergoing some kind of spiritual awakening, it is difficult for most people to grasp the reality of such invisible beings as gods or Buddhas. It is hard for us to assimilate them on the emotional level.

So it was that statues and paintings of the Buddhas became objects of veneration. All sorts of Buddhist stories were told. But these do not necessarily express the essence of the religion. The statue or painting of the Buddha resting with dignity in the temple is a ship to carry suffering people to the far shore of peace and tranquillity, a lantern to bring light to a dark place. Such icons are perceived as beneficent beings, reaching out to us confused, lost ones, taking our hands, and leading us in the right direction. That is why we join our hands in prayer, bow our heads, and give thanks before such images.

But that is not our goal. The true reality that Shinran conceived of, the place to which all people would eventually be led, was the state of the Pure Land, beyond all images. The True Pure Land sect, which was founded by Shinran and later popularized by Rennyo, called this primary object of faith and worship the *myogo* (name). This name was six or eight or sometimes ten Chinese characters written on a piece of paper, and this was worshipped. Most *myogo* consisted of the characters Na-mu-A-mi-da-bu-tsu, or "I take refuge in Amida Buddha."

What does it mean to worship these written words and what relationship do these words bear to our own suffering? Shinran's Buddha was the concept "Namu Amida Butsu," and that idea is not like a concrete Buddha that can be seen with the eye. The state of Pure Land is, like faith itself, invisible. A world on an infinite scale.

It is eternal time—something that has transcended all concepts of time. This is what Shinran expressed in the words "Amida Buddha."

Namu means to take refuge in. Taking refuge in something means to kneel before it, bow our heads, give ourselves to it completely, and vow to unite ourselves with it. Rennyo developed Shinran's *nembutsu* of taking refuge in the Buddha to a *nembutsu* that was an expression of joy and gratitude at encountering the Buddha, and it was that form that he popularized.

Fuller explanations of the *nembutsu* can be found in any introductory book on True Pure Land Buddhism. I have only explained it roughly and in brief, leaving out the reasoning and presenting only the conclusions.

Instead of chanting "Namu Amida Butsu" or "Namo Amida Butsu," clearly enunciating each syllable, many elderly Japanese say "Namandabu" or even "Namanda," but these are just abbreviated versions of the original formula. Chanting "Namanda" is in complete accord with Shinran's intent. He wasn't directing his gaze at any visual image but at the Pure Land, an invisible, infinite, and unlimited realm that stands in opposition to the realm of rational, scientific thought. To my way of thinking, the realms generally known as heaven and hell are merely points of passage on the way to that Pure Land.

There's no need to be bound to this phrase, however. Many Japanese find it very old-fashioned. You might just as well chant something that expresses your devotion and gratitude to a power beyond your own. In this terrible world of ours, all that counts is that you mentally clasp your hands in gratitude and say your thanks for being alive. Do this every day; do this to keep yourself aware and open whether you are in the grip of terrible suffering or are experiencing boundless joy.

What Was the Source of Honen's Self-assurance?

The teaching of Honen that has made the deepest impression on me is "the easy practice of the *nembutsu*" (*igyo nembutsu*). I think of this as "birth in the Pure Land through the easy practice" (*igyo ojo*). Of Shinran's teachings, the doctrine of *jinen honi* seems the most profound. Among the concepts found in Rennyo's teachings I am especially drawn to *tariki hongan*.

I think these three concepts shed different kinds of light on what is essentially the same reality. Beyond them all reverberates "There is nothing I can do," the voice of the Other Power that I discussed at the beginning of this book.

"Easy practice" is used in contrast to "difficult practices" such as asceticism and study. The term *ojo* (birth in the Pure Land) is used today in Japan to mean death, attaining Buddhahood, or being reborn in the Pure Land of Perfect Bliss, but I give it a slightly different interpretation.

I interpret *ojo* to mean "providing the strength to live," "feeling the joy of life," and "a sense of true peace even though one still endures suffering and anxiety."

To those who were desperately seeking birth in the Pure Land in his day, Honen said that there was no need to engage in difficult study or strict, difficult practices. All they had to do was believe in the Buddha and chant the *nembutsu*. That was all, and they would be saved without fail. His words were filled with self-assurance. In the context of the Buddhist world of the time, this was a radical, even scandalous declaration, and Honen eventually found himself in serious trouble for his beliefs. Several of his disciples were arrested and executed, and both he and Shinran were exiled.

But Honen continued to insist that the *nembutsu* was all that was necessary. There was no need for other practices. Just chant "Namu Amida Butsu."

What gave Honen the confidence to speak this way? He insisted that anyone who had exclusive faith in the Buddha and chanted the *nembutsu* would be born in the Pure Land, but there was no objective proof of the truth of this claim.

Yet, there was a good reason that Honen could preach this with such self-assurance. I believe it was because Honen himself had been saved through the easy practice of the *nembutsu*. No doubt he, an individual with many personal sufferings living in a hard world, actually experienced a strength to live, a joy of living, and a peace in life through the simple, exclusive practice of the *nembutsu*, without difficult study or strenuous ascetic practice.

That is why Honen so arduously advocated the easy practice for birth in the Pure Land, and why his teachings moved and influenced so many others. The youthful Shinran was one of those who entrusted himself to Honen's promises.

I have used the word "entrusted." In Buddhist terminology, this is "to take refuge" (*kie suru*). Taking refuge implies not only having faith but abandoning all petty calculations and giving one's entire being to someone or something.

Shinran then carried this a step further.

The Experience of a Great, Invisible Power

Honen said that all we had to do was to recite the *nembutsu*. The *nembutsu*, of course, is "Namu Amida Butsu." *Namu* is a Chinese transliteration of the Sanskrit word *namas*. *Namo* is another form of the same root word, and both *namas* and *namo* express respect and trust. The common Hindi greeting still used today, *Namaste*, derives from the same root. *Te* means "you."

Namas is translated into Japanese as *kie*, which means, as we have seen, "to take refuge in." It means to kneel before the Buddha, lower one's head in respect, and express one's faith in the Buddha. We can think of *Namu* as an expression of the thought "I leave everything to you."

Who is that "you"? It is Amida Buddha.

Amida also comes from Sanskrit. It is a Chinese transliteration of two words, *Amitayus* and *Amitabha*. *Amitayus* was translated into Chinese as "infinite life," and *Amitabha* as "infinite light." *Amitayus* represents the infinite life force that pulses throughout the entire universe, and *Amitabha* is the light of truth that illuminates the entire world without exception.

Finally, *Butsu* is Buddha, a word that means "the awakened one." It refers to one who has profoundly awakened with his entire being to the great, invisible power of the universe.

Eventually it came to be used as a name for Shakyamuni, who of course was an example of such an awakened being, but originally there were many Buddhas.

I regard Amida Buddha as a characterization of the infinite life force and the light of truth, created to make these ideas accessible to the masses. Once put into this narrative form, the invisible force of the universe takes on a life and power that can reach and communicate to us.

Honen, founder of the Pure Land sect, enthusiastically taught the *nembutsu* as a means to experience the invisible power of the universe and illuminate the darkness of our world.

It Comes to Us

There is an easy way to be born in the Pure Land. Just concentrate on chanting the *nembutsu*, says Honen. Shinran took refuge in Honen's teaching, but he carried it to an even deeper level.

It is easy, thought Shinran, to simply recite the *nembutsu* vocally, but it is much harder to take refuge in the Buddha, honestly and without reservations, as a child might. "Without reservations" means discarding all our preconceived notions and knowledge. We must become like an innocent child, and that is a difficult thing to do.

Further, taking refuge is not something one decides to do consciously and achieves through some effort. Instead, one is naturally drawn toward it by the great power itself.

The words "There is nothing I can do" are, I think, a perfect expression of this.

One recites the *nembutsu:* "Namu Amida Butsu." This is not an act of bowing before the Buddha and vowing one's faith in him. It is not a conscious effort to abandon your previous self.

No, one is spontaneously drawn to the point where one cannot help but do this. How does this happen?

One hears that there is a great monk named Honen. This is the first act of the invisible power. One has heard about the great monk, but one doesn't have the opportunity to go and listen to what he has to say. Then a good friend or a family member tells you that Honen is preaching today and invites you to go along and listen to him. What was it that caused you to pick up this book? That, too, may be an act of the power, coming toward you from the other side.

You hear Honen's voice, you see his face, and you are moved—you don't know why—by what he says. You cannot suppress the desire that rises up within you to follow him. This is not something you consciously tried to do, or something someone else persuaded you to do. This opportunity was revealed to you by an invisible light.

This is the point of the great transformation from Self-Power to Other Power.

The words "There is nothing I can do" are always echoing in the depths of my mind.

"What will be, will be," I think, and in my heart I nod in assent: "What should be, will be." When I do this, a wondrous sense of security comes upon me from somewhere. Although my heart was racing painfully just a moment before, it begins to calm down. I am still floundering, but I am no longer at my heart's mercy.

I feel as if I hear Shinran saying quietly, "There is nothing I can do."

"The Banisher of Grief"

Shinran was a very interesting person. Once when he attended a funeral he found the deceased's loved ones crowded around the body, weeping and lamenting. A monk there scolded them. "This person is now entering the Pure Land, wrapped in light. You weep and lament because your faith is weak. You should be rejoicing that he has entered the Pure Land!"

"There are always stupid monks," said Shinran in the record of his words and deeds called the *Kudensho*. "And he was wrong." When asked what he would have done, Shinran replied, "Drink is also known as 'Banisher of Grief.' You should give them enough sake to make them laugh, and then leave." Give those who are grieving for the deceased enough sake so that they forget their sadness and begin recounting their memories of the loved one. When they are drunk and begin to make jokes, get up and leave. That is the proper way to conduct a funeral, says Shinran.

I love this episode. I think it shows Shinran's very human side peeping out from his otherwise relentless spiritual logic.

People are born with four things that are not subject to their will: birth, old age, sickness, and death. We cannot control our birth, nor can we control aging or sickness, much less old age. Every person is fated to die from the moment of birth. When we realize this, we are bound to feel a fundamental, indescribable grief in our heart, our gut, our very bones.

IV. *Tariki*

The Realm of Other Power

In Japan, the term "Other Power" is most frequently heard in the phrase "the original vow of Other Power" (*tariki hongan*).

It is most often used to mean leaving things up to others, or depending on others—that is, the opposite of self-effort. For example, the phrase "personal responsibility" has become popular lately, and in defining it people frequently say it means that we mustn't rely on *tariki hongan.*

Of course, the fact that words change meaning over time cannot be avoided, but the original meaning of *tariki hongan* was most definitely not dependence on others or refusal to accept responsibility for one's actions or fate. Before I make an attempt to describe *tariki hongan,* I think it is important to point out that *tariki hongan* is a major philosophical concept rooted in an extremely powerful worldview, and it has served as a steadfast source of strength for those facing a crisis.

Tariki, as we have seen, means Other Power. *Hongan,* or "original vow," is the very core of the teaching of Pure Land Buddhism. At the start of his practice to become a Buddha, the Bodhisattva Dharmakara made forty-eight vows that he promised to realize when he attained enlightenment. Many of the vows are about the Pure Land—a symbolic description of the state of enlightenment—that he would create when he became a Buddha. Of all those vows, Dharmakara's "original" or essential vow is his promise, once he has attained enlightenment and become Amida Buddha, that any living being who calls out his name will be born into his Pure Land and attain enlightenment. This is the vow that became the core teaching of Pure Land Buddhism.

Although relying on "the original vow of Other power" may seem to mean depending on another (Amida) for one's salvation, it is really a much more radical idea. Since Dharmakara has already achieved enlightenment and become Amida, it follows that *we are all already enlightened.* The true Pure Land teaching, then, is not to gain birth in the Pure Land by chanting the Buddha's name (that would be Self-Power, after all) but realizing, from the bottom of one's being, that one is already enlightened. The intense gratitude one feels after experiencing this spiritual revelation is expressed in the cry *Namu Amida Butsu*. What makes Pure Land Buddhism such a radical philosophy is that what at first appears to be a means to attain enlightenment (chanting Amida's name) is simultaneously the activity of enlightenment itself. *Tariki hongan* is a philosophy that transcends time; it leaps over all boundaries, and in chanting the Buddha's name past and future are one, practice and attainment are one, suffering and enlightenment are one. It is not a philosophy of passivity and irresponsibility, as the phrase has come to be interpreted in Japan over the centuries. It is a philosophy of radical spiritual activity, of personal, existential revolution.

Many people may think it odd to call Other Power a philosophical concept or worldview, but since it is the foundation of the Buddhism of Honen, founder of the Pure Land sect of Japanese Buddhism, as well as of Shinran, the founder of the True Pure Land sect, and his disciple Rennyo, there can be no denying the importance of this idea.

The reason that I have not used the word "faith" in discussing *tariki hongan* is that I am convinced that *tariki,* or Other Power, has an intense power to move the hearts of people today, a power that transcends sectarian or theological distinctions.

Tariki has the power to move all of us whether or not we believe in the existence of God or the Buddha, whether or not we accept the existence of a world we can't see, a realm transcending all national and ethnic boundaries. I also believe that this realm of Other Power is that "special something" we are all unconsciously seeking.

I would like to now explore a little further my own understanding of Other Power, which was passed to my ears by the voices of others.

"Doing What Man Can Do Is Heaven's Will"

"The *ji* of *jinen* means 'spontaneity,'" says Shinran.

"*Nen* means 'what should be,'" he writes.

Honi is the unseen power that operates on us. We tend to think that we make decisions, judgments, and efforts to achieve something, but that isn't really the case.

Tariki hongan describes the same reality as Shinran's *jinen honi.*

For a long time, I misunderstood the meaning of *tariki,* or Other Power. A young critic said to me, "Mr. Itsuki, you often speak of *tariki,* but in order to really have an awareness of Other Power, don't you need to make some use of Self-Power?"

"Maybe that's true," I said.

When I used to explain Other Power, I often used the example of a yacht. A yacht without an engine cannot sail when there is absolutely no wind. If there's even the slightest breeze, it can sail, but with none, it's useless. It doesn't make any difference what you do to the yacht. Without the wind of Other Power, our daily lives, too, cannot be made to sail along.

But even if the wind blows, it may catch you napping if your sails are furled, and you'll miss your chance to get moving. That's why it's important to make an effort to remain alert, no matter how long the doldrums persist, and watch the sky and wait patiently for the wind's arrival.

If you think of this effort as Self-Power, then, as my young critic noted, a certain degree of Self-Power is necessary.

However, recently I have become convinced that what appears to be the effort of Self-Power in this scenario is actually the activity of Other Power.

It is nothing but Other Power that gives the sailor the power to make the effort to wait for the wind without giving up, and the alertness to be prepared for its arrival; it also gives him the unbending faith that eventually the wind will blow.

The essence of the working of Other Power is the spontaneous, wondrous force that gives us the will to act, that makes us "Do what man can do and then wait for heaven's will," as the saying goes.

I am purposely reading "Do what man can do and then wait for heaven's will" as "Doing what man can do is heaven's will," and for me "heaven's will" is Other Power. Deciding to do whatever it is possible to do and then carrying out that decision—this is not possible without a push from behind by Other Power. When you realize this, any thought that we are doing things by our Self-Power seems positively comic.

There are also times when I surprise myself at the intensity of my effort. Looking back, I wonder what got into me. When that determination wells up from inside, "the wind of Other Power" is blowing.

When I demonstrate a strong decisiveness, courage, effort, and perseverance, when I make a 120-percent effort that astonishes even me, I think it is the light of Other Power shining through.

There are times when work doesn't go well, times when, no matter how hard I try, all I do is fail. At such times I say to myself, "It seems the wind of Other Power isn't blowing," and I shrug, without blaming myself.

On the other hand, there are times when things go much more smoothly than I had anticipated. I am praised, and I find my confidence growing. At such times, it is important to stop for a moment and quietly reflect.

"There is nothing I can do," I whisper softly to myself. A great, invisible, favorable wind is blowing, and its Other Power is making things go far more smoothly than I could ever hope to achieve by my own effort.

One should be humbly grateful to Other Power, and never be arrogant in regard to one's success. That is what makes the way of Other Power so very difficult.

Easy, Deep, and Wide

Shinran's disciple Rennyo was a man who devoted his life to spreading his master's true and correct teachings as broadly as possible among the people.

Rennyo is frequently criticized for vulgarizing Shinran's profound philosophy when he communicated it to the masses.

But as far as Other Power is concerned, I think it is a rare person who exemplified it so completely and vitally in his life as Rennyo.

Honen taught that the difficult practice of attaining birth in the Pure Land could be made easy. Shinran's task was to take this easy way his master taught and to pursue it more deeply. And Rennyo took Shinran's deep faith and devoted his life to propagating it widely among the people.

Through this triple process of making the difficult easy, the easy deep, and the deep wide, Japanese Buddhism has been able to endure in the hearts of the people.

Shinran's thought reached the point where he declared that "The supreme Buddha has no form." Amida Buddha, ultimately, is "a means of expressing That Which Is."

A Buddha in any form, whether a statue or a painting, is a narrative representation, a visual means of expression only. Behind the image is *jinen honi,* the infinite life force of the universe and the light of truth that illuminates all existence.

Rennyo, on the other hand, in his single-minded concentration on the masses, strongly emphasized a different narrative, that of *tariki hongan.* His Amida Buddha is a compassionate figure who cannot abandon the suffering, the discriminated against, the lowly, and women and children.

His Buddha finds it impossible to refuse to save the suffering multitudes; he bears the full weight of their burden of sadness, so heavy that he cannot stand up. No matter what secure and lofty position awaits him, he is a strange Buddha who is fated to be unable to forget the foolish humans on Earth. He calls out to them as long as his voice lasts, he extends both hands to grasp those of all sentient beings. This is called his "great compassion" (*daihi*); it is also his "original vow" (*hongan*).

Amida Buddha suffers together with humanity. He cannot be saved until they are. In this sense he is a tragic Buddha, a pitiful Buddha.

Rennyo, too, called out to the suffering people until his throat was raw, "Can't you hear his voice? Can't you feel the warmth of the Buddha's hand?" He must have been aware that he was following the example of the Buddha when he preached.

Without question, it was none other than the wind of Other Power that propelled him along as he continued to preach *tariki hongan*.

Learning by Listening

All of us have had memories burned into our brains from before we were fully conscious. We never made an effort to remember them. They entered our minds through our skin.

After growing up, after growing old, these memories come back to us. We smile and wonder, "Why do I remember something like this?" But these memories have continued to live, quietly, secretly, deep in our hearts, for all those years.

I really don't remember much of what I have studied since I became an adult, but things engraved in my mind when I was a child come back to me as time passes with a freshness that astonishes me.

One of the old, old memories that rises out of the depths of my being is the following passage:

Kimyo muryoju nyorai
Namu fukashigi ko

Hozo Bosatsu inni ji
Zaise jizai obutsu sho

(Taking refuge in the Tathagata Amitayus
I praise his limitless light
When Dharmakara Bodhisattava had not yet attained
   enlightenment
He dwelled in the place of the Buddha's freedom.)

I never consciously memorized this. I have no memory of it at all. One day, in my late forties, I found myself repeating this. At the same time, I remembered these lines:

Since Amida Buddha attained enlightenment
Ten *kalpas* have passed
The halo of the Dharma body, without limit
Illuminates the blind ignorance of this world

The first passage is part of the famous "true faith verse" *(shoshinge)* from Shinran's great work *Kyogyoshinsho* (Teaching, practice, faith, and attainment), appearing at the end of the section on "Practice." The second passage is one of the poems in Shinran's collection called *Wasan* (Japanese poems). I can't help but think that it's very odd indeed that these strange, poetic phrases should remain in my memory.

This is my theory: When I was a boy in Korea, my family, like all Japanese families living outside Japan, had a Buddhist altar. My parents were schoolteachers and every morning they would sit in front of the altar and, placing their hands together, chant something.

I recall the golden light of the candles, the gentle ring of the bell, and my mother or father softly repeating something. A light trace of incense rising from somewhere. Hearing those voices day after day, the words must have seeped into my young mind like water seeping into sand.

It was none other than Rennyo who invented the morning worship ceremony of the True Pure Land sect and established it among his followers. He combined the passage from the "true faith verse," the *nembutsu,* and the Japanese poem from the *Wasan* into a service to be recited morning and evening. Gradually people adopted it and made it a part of the rhythm of their life.

That ceremony that Rennyo invented five hundred years ago had been passed all the way down to me, as a child, in a colony far from Japan. Although I had no idea that these words were composed by Shinran, although I had no idea of their meaning, they entered the deepest recesses of my young mind and there they remain to this day. Without knowing it, I keep Rennyo's legacy alive.

When we realize that hundreds of thousands—no, millions—of the ordinary people have handed this Buddhism down from generation to generation, as part of their lives, their very beings, we can't but be impressed by the breadth and weight of what Rennyo has left us.

Two Factors That Shaped Rennyo's Life

When Rennyo was born, his father, Zonnyo, was only twenty years old. He did not have a home of his own, and he could not officially marry. Rennyo's mother was a serving girl at Honganji.

Honganji, Rennyo's home, began as a monument to Shinran. Called the Otani Mieido, it was his tomb, built by the donations of his followers in eastern Japan. In the early years, Shinran's youngest daughter, Kakushin, was appointed caretaker, and the temple buildings were the common property of Shinran's followers. At this time, the caretaker was elected after consulting carefully with those followers.

As time passed, a hereditary system evolved and eventually Honganji was established as the head temple of the True Pure Land sect. The temple was still very poor, however, and accounts from the period describe a desolate place in terrible disrepair.

There are several different theories regarding Rennyo's mother's role at Honganji. Some say she was a maid of Zonnyo's grandmother, others just a common servant. Another theory has it that she was of the untouchable class. Whichever theory is correct, she was clearly of such a social class that Zonnyo was not permitted to take her as an official wife.

On his father's side, Rennyo was a descendant of Shinran and thus of the aristocracy; on his mother's he was of low social status. When Rennyo was six, something happened that changed his life forever: His father officially married. This meant, of course, that Rennyo's mother had to leave the temple. Zonnyo's new wife, a well-born young women who had served in the household of a leading feudal lord, could not be expected to live side-by-side with a low-class serving woman who had borne her husband's child. These two opposing factors were to play a part in Rennyo's character development and influence his entire life. In my opinion, they created an interesting combination of pride and a strong identity with the lower classes.

His aristocratic pride and self-confidence were key factors in his successful effort to establish Honganji firmly as a spiritual and secular power and to preserve Shinran's lineage for the ages. This side of his personality is especially conspicuous in his later years.

On the other hand, his identification with the lower classes manifested itself as a very strong sympathy and personal warmth that contrasted with the cool intellectualism of Shinran and his teachings.

Shinran's interpretation of "comrades in faith," for example, was not simply a brotherhood of those who had taken refuge in the Buddha and chanted the *nembutsu*. It was an expression of a more rigorous religious logic. It pointed to an absolute equality of all those who believed in salvation by the Buddha and had felt the illumination of Other Power, regardless of their social position.

In contrast, Rennyo's view of this comradeship was very emotional and passionate and personal. Rennyo carried Shinran's faith into the world, into society, with all its confusion and contradiction. By doing so, he exposed himself to the temptations and corruption of that society. But if he had not done so, the True Pure Land teaching of "evil people as the true object of salvation" *(akunin shoki)* would have been nothing but empty words. Though born in a temple from a family of monks, Rennyo shouldered that contradiction bravely and made it his own.

Rennyo resided at Honganji for fourteen years. He was not the heir, and surely his life was very constrained. He married and had one child after another. He had to send them out in service to other temples just to feed them. The Honganji servants were forced to eat the offerings to the Buddha, and the family diluted their soup so that one bowl fed three.

On many days, Rennyo ate only one meal, and he often went for days without eating at all.

The Buddha Saves Evil People First

The doctrine of "evil people as the true object of salvation" *(akunin shoki)* is usually thought of as having originated in a work called *Tannisho* (Lamenting heresies), a record of Shinran's words by his disciple Yuien.

Recently, however, several scholars have emphasized that, in fact, *akunin shoki* was a teaching transmitted to Shinran by his teacher

Honen. It doesn't make any difference to me. In the broader view, *akunin shoki* is an idea that can be seen throughout Mahayana Buddhist history in both India and China. At any rate, a passage from the *Kudensho,* a record of oral teachings in the True Pure Land sect, states "The original vow of the Thus-Come One is for ordinary people, not saints."

Allow me to quote at length from the *Kudensho:*

Nyoshin Shonin once said this. It is frequently thought that, since Amida Buddha's compassion is so infinite in its embrace it even includes evil people, surely it is only natural that people who are performing good deeds should be saved. But this is a betrayal of the meaning of the Buddha's vow and Shakyamuni's noble words. Just think about it. Didn't the Buddha vow to save first and foremost those who are living sad lives full of pain and suffering? The fortunate people are his second priority. Since the Buddha even saves these fortunate (good) people, it's only natural that he should save the all-important evil people first. People often say that the Buddha saves even evil people, so of course he saves the good, but that is wrong. It's the other way around: He saves even good people, so of course he saves the evil. This is the teaching that Shinran received directly from his teacher Honen: Evil people are the true object of salvation, good people are secondary. This, said Nyoshin, is an extremely important teaching.

Jitsuen Kakehashi, in his book *Shinran,* has also written on this subject. This is an excellent, clear introduction to the subject, and I would like to quote from his explanation of the subject, which I find very convincing. The passage below is from his chapter "The Oral Teachings Received from Honen."

The doctrine of "evil people as the true object of salvation" was first communicated not in written form but orally, from Honen to Shinran and then Shinran to Yuien. Before the Pure

Land teachings were widely known, such complex teachings could be easily misunderstood, and so they were only transmitted orally, to a disciple, with a full explanation to avoid misinterpretation. Kakunyo's *Kudensho* tells us that "Nyoshin states that Shinran received this teaching from Honen," in other words, that the doctrine of "evil people as the true object of salvation" was passed down from Honen to Shinran to Nyoshin (Shinran's grandson and Kakunyo's teacher).

We know this was originally Honen's teaching because in the Daigo edition of his biography we find the passage "Since even good people will attain birth in the Pure Land, of course evil people will." Next to this passage is a note in small writing that says "This is in the oral transmission." This supports the claim of the *Kudensho* that the doctrine of "evil people as the true object of salvation" originated with Honen.

In other words, many important ideas and precious words in the Buddhist tradition have been kept alive in people's hearts, passed from one to another, master to disciple, so that it is very difficult to tell where they originated.

I once saw a television documentary that searched for the source of the Ganges River by traveling all the way up into the glaciers of the Himalayas. But it is impossible to identify that first drop of water melting from the timeless snows of the Himalayas. The glaciers are born from snow, from fog, from clouds, from evaporation, and the river's source can never be found.

What We Look For in Religion

For me, the "evil people" in the doctrine of "evil people as the true object of salvation" are people who have had hard lives filled with suffering. Jesus gave his unqualified love to the sick, the poor, the lowly. It is only natural that such people should be the first whom Amida Buddha embraces with his limitless compassion.

Even though I might be bitterly unhappy in my personal life and might be calling out the Buddha's name from the bottom of my heart, I remain a second—or even third—priority. Those who have wealth, fame, and power in our world are not the real objects of salvation.

It would be unfair. It's unfair for those who have a pleasant life in this world to also have a pleasant life in the next. When Honen and Shinran were alive, people believed that hell really existed. Of course, some people also believed in paradise, but not as a place that ordinary people had any prospect of experiencing. It was believed that only the aristocracy or the wealthy, those who could carry out arduous religious practice, or build temples, or make huge donations, or sponsor prayers by high-ranking monks, had a passport to paradise.

Naturally, for the many, many people who were doing their best just to survive and had no time for such good works, the anxiety of their awaiting hell played a much larger role than any expectation of birth in paradise. And of course those who were scorned by the world—the merchants, craftsmen, artists, prostitutes, fishermen, hunters, horse drivers, cart pullers, boatmen, sailors, and beggars—had no expectation that they would ever see paradise.

Here is the secret to the power of religion: It says that these will be the first people to be saved.

Isn't this the source of religion's power—the wish that those who are blessed in this world will suffer in the next, and those who suffer in this world will be blessed in the next?

But that is too baldly put. It's not beautiful. Let's rephrase it. The essence of religion should be a warm light for those who in this world have little happiness, are starved for love and loving, who sweat and bleed more than their fair share.

I think, however, that Honen and Shinran used the words "evil people" in a way far more complex than my own, simple definition.

A Volcanic Force in an Age of Crisis

The fifteenth century, the time in which Rennyo lived and preached, was a time of war, famine, violent uprisings, and epidemics, an age in which a bottomless feeling of the world's impermanence threatened to swallow the people's hearts. It is often compared to our present times.

In this context, Rennyo fought against two powerful enemies. One was the near-dormant religious establishment. It had acquired great wealth over the centuries as a recipient of large estates from the nobility and warrior classes, and lived in complacent contentment.

The other enemy was the newly arisen religious cults, of which there were many different kinds.

For example, one such cult took Shinran's teaching of *akunin shoki,* that evil people were the proper object of salvation, and distorted it. This cult taught that the more evil deeds one committed, the more certain one was of being born in the Pure Land. Groups who purposely committed evil acts appeared, believing that this would assure them of the Buddha's salvation.

There were also cults that worshipped individuals as living Buddhas with superhuman powers. There were cults that promised forgiveness of sins for a fee, rewards in the afterlife based on contributions in this life. Other cults conducted strange initiation rites at midnight deep in the mountains.

These sham religions spread like an epidemic among the people, shaken as they were by feelings of impermanence and hopelessness.

Isn't this precisely our present situation?

Rennyo fought against the lazy established religions while at the same time confronting the newly arisen cults head-on. In less trying times, Rennyo might have been a rather ordinary, even common man. But when he faced a crisis, he showed himself to be a very different person, flashing with powerful brilliance. He declared unequivocally, "Shinran's teaching of *akunin shoki* does not mean it is all right to do evil." It was a mighty struggle.

After Rennyo had successfully built up his groups of *nembutsu* followers, the samurai leaders of the period could no longer ignore this new force. Some tried to suppress the *nembutsu* followers, while others attempted to form alliances with them. In Rennyo's later years he faced the difficult problem of conflict and compromise with the warrior government. Rennyo's eighty-five years of life were indeed filled with drama.

There was another side of Rennyo that has endeared him to me and many other Japanese. Rennyo never ignored people's passionate feelings, their sadness and tears. He was the kind of person who could not overlook an unhappy fellow human being, who flew to his side and wept with him, who couldn't help expressing his emotions in the form of the *nembutsu*. He knew how powerful such things could be. I think Rennyo's personal portion of tragedy in life was also immeasurable.

Shinran would have been a forceful, fascinating presence in any age, but Rennyo was a man whose volcanic force was especially felt in an age of crisis.

Rennyo's Letters

There is a limit to the power of words in describing religious faith, but Rennyo came up with a new medium of sorts: his letters, which are known as the *Ofumi* or *Gobunsho* in Japanese. Rennyo wrote these letters as messages to his followers.

The letters contain detailed instructions concerning both matters of faith, such as how to hold religious gatherings, and more practical matters regarding the defense of the True Pure Land sect, such as how to react to persecution from local warriors and feudal lords.

When the village leader received a letter from Rennyo, he would call all the local followers together in a meeting called a *ko* (literally, lecture). At this religious gathering on the village level, he would read the letter aloud. By doing so, Rennyo's thoughts were conveyed simultaneously to dozens of others.

The listeners would memorize the letter and return to their even more local settlement and pass on Rennyo's message again. Sometimes the letters were copied and then sent on to another *ko* or group of followers.

Some followers who possessed copies of Rennyo's letters would recite them every morning and evening, just as if they were Buddhist sutras. In this way, Rennyo's teachings were transmitted to the next generation, and the Honganji organization grew by leaps and bounds. It was just this substantial worldly success in expanding Honganji that no doubt resulted in the criticism and attack that has been directed at Rennyo.

One of the things that Rennyo repeatedly insisted upon in his letters was the importance of speaking out.

The farmers and fishermen of Rennyo's day were like a great, silent mass of sand. "Talking only makes the lips cold," went the saying, and in truth, one false word, one word of criticism of the ruling class, could result in the speedy loss of one's head. It was the custom of the lower classes to toil silently like ants, and take care not to say anything unnecessary. Rennyo addressed this mass of people who had forgotten how to say anything that wasn't necessary, telling them to gather those who were interested in the *nembutsu* they practiced. Start by getting together in the homes of village leaders or those sympathetic to your cause, he said.

He was telling these people, who started working when the stars were still shining in the skies and continued long after dark, only to return to their homes and collapse like exhausted beasts of burden on a bed of straw, to make some personal time, to make time to chant *nembutsu,* to create a place where they could talk about their faith, about Buddhism. This place where they could speak about and share their faith took shape as the institution of the *ko.*

In this way, the laboring class found, for the first time, a place where they could talk not about such practical matters as when to plant the crops or how to parcel out the irrigation water but about their spiritual lives. And in that new place they began to talk about religious and philosophical matters—What is paradise? Is the *nembutsu* really effective?—and to share their experiences of faith.

Rennyo's message was that a silent person is a bad person, a silent person won't attain Buddhahood. He urged those who had lost their ability to express their wishes, their hopes, their feelings, to find their voices and speak out. In his letters, Rennyo repeatedly told his followers not to speak out simply as individuals but to get together in large numbers, to debate, to talk to each other, and thereby open the true way of the *nembutsu.*

This was a very novel and creative approach for a religious leader at that time.

Rennyo-san

The Buddhism of the Kamakura period, which includes that of Honen and Shinran, arose as a Buddhism dedicated to the salvation of the people, the masses, as opposed to the Buddhism of earlier times, which was intimately linked with the interests of the state and the aristocratic class.

But Honen still lived as a monk, observing the Buddhist precepts and living a "pure" life. He was a member of the aristocracy, and the aura of a high-ranking, aristocratic monk emanates from him. His disciple Shinran described himself as "neither monk nor laity." He was not a monk; yet, he also drew a line between his way of life and a completely secular one. He remained a wandering philosopher, a seeker of truth, his entire life.

Rennyo was different from both Honen and Shinran. He leapt right into the middle of the troubled waters of secular life and the world of the masses. He did this in order to bring his single-minded faith in Shinran's teachings as the only way of salvation to as many people as possible. There is, of course, a contradiction here. In that sense, Rennyo's position is quite different from Shinran's "neither monk nor laity."

Rennyo was aware of that contradiction, I believe, and was prepared to sacrifice himself to achieve his aim. It was impossible to spread Shinran's very personal, individually oriented teachings to large numbers of people without transforming their purity, their radical absolutism. Rennyo started on this path when he wrote, "Distill the hundred into ten and the ten into one." Yet, this is by no means an error.

Difficult philosophies and complex arguments have an independent existence, a substance of their own. The moment we try to simplify them and express them in a way that all can understand, we have transformed them and created something else.

Yet, the "easy practice of the *nembutsu*" that Honen and Shinran advocated was a practice based on the compassion of the Buddha to save all living beings.

I think that when Rennyo decided to sacrifice his salvation to spread Shinran's teachings, he was already prepared to go to hell.

Even Shinran had written, "Hell is my determined home." Rennyo had an even stronger awareness of his spiritual shortcomings, and it would not be at all strange for him to have accepted hell as his future home.

When Rennyo decided to spread Shinran's teachings throughout the world and to rebuild Honganji as a citadel of Buddhism in a world of chaos and strife, he was fully prepared to submerge himself completely in the secular world.

In the early summer of 1953, when I was a junior in university, I visited Kanazawa. It was just around the time that the Korean War was coming to an end. At the time, the attention of all Japan was focused on a place called Uchinada, near Kanazawa on the Japan Sea. The governments of Japan and the United States had unilaterally decided to make the sandy dunes along the sea a permanent U.S. military firing range. The local residents opposed this decision and were staging a sit-in to protest it. There was such unified opposition that even women, the elderly, and children joined the demonstration. As live shells and ammunition fell all around them, they sat there at the risk of their lives. The astounding unity and strength of shared purpose demonstrated by the farmers and fishermen made quite an impression on the Japanese people as a whole.

I happened to be visiting Kanazawa at this time, and I also went to Uchinada, carried along by the sea of reporters and supporters of the strike from all across Japan. I realize now that there was a complex political power struggle taking place; at the time I found the fierce head-on resistance of the local residents to the actions of the Japanese and U.S. governments quite inspiring.

I remember that a student of Kanazawa University who was with me then commented, "The Kaga region has a tradition of local resistance. *Nembutsu* uprisings (*ikko ikki*) took place here, after all." That was the first I had heard of this, and it was from that time that I began to think about the *nembutsu* uprisings.

I will discuss the uprisings further below, but I think we can see Rennyo's influence in them, in various ways. Whatever he may have intended, it cannot be denied that the seeds of faith that he planted were the trigger that released the tremendous explosion of the *nembutsu* uprisings.

Ten years after my visit, I ended up living in Kanazawa for a time, and I came to realize anew the profound connection between Rennyo and the climate and geography of what is called the Hokuriku region, the prefectures of Toyama, Ishikawa, and Fukui along the Japan Sea.

Hokuriku is often called the Pure Land sect kingdom. Rennyo flowed like groundwater through the lives of the people who lived there, and there were many stories and fables told about him. It is the same today. The image of Rennyo in Hokuriku is not that of an elevated, saintly figure, but of a very human man, as close to his followers as a family member.

He is usually called not "Saint Rennyo" but just "Rennyo-san," and is spoken of with warm familiarity.

One of the local legends is about Rennyo's tooth, a humorous account of how when Rennyo was visiting a place in the area called Matsuoka, one of his front teeth happened to fall out. One of his followers picked it up and preserved it, and now it sits enshrined in the local temple as one of its "treasures."

There are countless such stories centered around Rennyo, and certainly no other figure is as revered or talked about in the Hokuriku region. I used to frequent a little hot-pot restaurant called Taro along the banks of the Asano River. The "granny" who was its proprietress has passed away now, but she used to tell me lots of the old stories about "Rennyo-san"—this "Rennyo-san" referring not to the man but the local festival that was held to commemorate his death. According to her, it was a holiday that the local craftsmen, the shop clerks, and the female factory workers looked forward to with feverish anticipation and excitement. They would gather at a hill in Kanazawa called Utatsuyama and have a boisterous time.

In the 1920s, it became the town's major festival, and was livelier than ever, with outdoor food stalls and samisen and drum performances—Rennyo's benign, invisible presence reigning over this popular celebration.

Straddling a Giant Contradiction

When people hear the name of Shinran, they unconsciously sit up straight and assume an expression of reverence and respect, but when Rennyo is mentioned they smile as if a fresh spring breeze has just wafted by. Although during temple ceremonies they bow respectfully, when it's over you will hear people making teasing and even grousing remarks.

When I called Rennyo a "strange person," I meant that he is a man with a strangely powerful attraction. I think this is partly because he is a problematic person. But it is precisely that contradiction, that difficulty, that makes him so interesting to me as a person.

Just as Shinran gave his soul completely to his master, Honen, Rennyo gave his entire being to his master, Shinran. He studied

Shinran's teachings and firmly dedicated himself to the only way of faith, as he understood it. He was born in an age when Shinran's thought was in danger of being corrupted and forgotten, and he called out with all his might for a return to Shinran.

But the more he tried to propagate Shinran's faith to the suffering masses of the people, the nameless men and women struggling at society's periphery, the more he found himself confronting a giant contradiction. This contradiction between thought and action, theory and practice, is always there, lying in wait for us.

Shinran walked a straight, unwavering path in the pursuit of personal faith and personal salvation. He was a single torch in the darkness. He can fairly be described as the founder of personal faith in Japan, of religion as an individual spiritual commitment. He was essentially a seeker of the way.

Rennyo was different. He tried to pass the torch of pure faith that Shinran lit to as many of the infinite number of people moaning in the darkness as he could. He worked desperately to keep that torch, wavering in the storm, from being extinguished.

Rennyo plunged into the world of strife and delusion, the dark and cloudy ocean where good and evil battle each other. It was an immeasurably secular world. Of course his path veered back and forth. When he sighted a perilous reef, he changed course and sent the ship in another direction. There are times when to take one step forward, one must take two back.

Rennyo's path was different than Shinran's. It was twisted and bumpy. At times he compromised, and at times he grandstanded, but at all times he kept up the fight, in his own way. If Shinran is a seeker of the Way, Rennyo is a propagator of the Way. Both of them sought the same truth, but walked a different route to reach it. Rennyo provided the masses of Japan's medieval period with an identity within a religious community.

In his later years, Rennyo built the Honganji into an institution before which even the great feudal lords of the period quaked. He was a success story who accomplished his goals and won fame and recognition in his lifetime.

Shinran's thought has a thoroughgoing modern intellectuality. It recalls the strict love of a father.

But Rennyo's words and deeds have a premodern, emotional,

popular appeal. They recall the so-called irrational love of a mother.

Rennyo is a giant contradiction.

Shadow Revealing Light

Honen, Shinran, and Rennyo were very much aware of the weight of the personal karma they each bore, their own foolishness, and the darkness in their hearts. This naturally led them to ask what such a person must do to live in the world and be saved in the Pure Land.

This clear awareness of the dark aspects of human existence led them to a knowledge of the light that illuminated them.

We cannot know that we are illuminated by a great light simply by looking up into the sky. But if we lower our heads and look down at our feet, we can clearly see the long, dark shadow that stretches out from us. We know that the darker and blacker that shadow is, the brighter is the light that shines upon us.

Shinran, and also Rennyo, told us to look at our own black shadow.

V. The Vital Spirit of *Menju*

Just Listen for One Thousand Days

It is usually assumed that deep, complex thoughts are best expressed in writing, but I have a different way of looking at it. I believe there are two kinds of words, words expressed in a living human voice and words expressed through writing. Content is important, no doubt, but I think the feeling communicated by the human voice is the life of words.

There is an old Japanese expression, *menju,* which translates as "face-to-face transmission," or, to adopt a now-popular term, "interfacing." Both these ideas mean to learn something, communicate something, or have something communicated at close personal range. Imagine two people sitting facing each other at a distance so short that they can hear each other breathing. This is *menju.*

In other words, *menju* proposes that a philosophy, a teaching, a faith, or any art in particular can only really be communicated, can only really be transmitted from one person to another, if they are within touching distance. The concept of *menju* has existed for a long time.

The founder of the Shingon sect of esoteric Buddhism in Japan, Kukai (774–835), went to China to study the new teachings of esoteric Buddhism, but he already had a thorough acquaintance with Buddhism, including esoteric Buddhism, before his trip. Why then did he travel all the way to China?

I believe that it was because he not only wanted to acquaint himself with the doctrines of the sect but also felt he needed the direct contact between master and disciple, *menju*. Kukai himself was able to spread the teachings of esoteric Buddhism in Japan after he returned because he had attained that all-important direct contact.

In direct contact, the expression of the speaker's face and voice, his breathing, his pauses, communicate at the same time as the content of the words, providing many added dimensions of meaning.

Let me tell you a story to illustrate this.

The Horyuji temple is located in Ikaruga, Japan. The writer and monk Nobutaka Ota in his book *Shin Horyuji Monogatari* (The new Horyuji story) provides an account of *menju* in this temple. I read this a long time ago, and I may not have it completely right, but let me present the rough outlines as I recall them.

Horyuji was from ancient times a temple for the advanced study of Buddhist doctrine. Join Saeki (1867–1952) was a famous monk of Horyuji who inherited this tradition and passed the torch on from the premodern to the modern period.

Saeki was born and raised near Horyuji. As a child, his name was Gakujiro (Little Student), and true to that name, he enjoyed studying. He was also very mischievous, and is said to have climbed over the walls of Horyuji and stolen persimmons from the temple garden. He later took the tonsure and went on to keep Horyuji's academic traditions alive, lecturing there for many years and playing a very important role in the history of Japanese Buddhism. A great many of the well-known monks in Nara and Kyoto studied under Saeki.

Saeki gave regular talks on Buddhism at Horyuji in the form of a sort of seminar. Ambitious young monks would attend, as would nuns from the adjacent Chuguji, who listened to his lectures from behind screens (since monks and nuns were not supposed to fraternize). Saeki's lectures must have been very profound. They were always held on schedule, come rain or shine.

Among those who came to hear his lectures was a certain young monk. He was a very serious young man who never missed a lecture. He listened to Saeki with his whole being, he both prepared and reviewed, and he did his best to learn, but he wasn't suited by nature for study and he had a difficult time grasping the essence of the Buddhist philosophy that Saeki presented in his lectures. He had more than a difficult time, actually; he utterly failed to understand.

Saeki, it is true, was lecturing on very difficult subjects. He had chosen the most complex of Buddhist philosophical systems, the Consciousness-Only school and the Abhidharma, or Kusha school. There is an old saying among monks, "Three years for Consciousness-Only and eight for Abhidharma," which just goes to show how difficult and abstruse they were—perhaps the equivalent of Jung and Freud, but with an even more detailed analysis of the worlds of consciousness and the unconscious. Many people had a hard time understanding these areas of Buddhist philosophy.

The young monk must have been a simple person. One day he suddenly appeared before Saeki and declared, "I have come to say farewell. I have carefully listened to your lectures every day, trying my best to understand them. But it seems that they are just beyond my ability, and I haven't been able to understand the important points. I think that I am just not suited to this kind of study, so I have decided to return to my village, plow the fields, and inherit my father's temple when the time comes. Thank you for your kindness all this time."

Saeki listened intently to the young monk's farewell speech, then said softly, "Just listen for one thousand days."

That comes to about three years. Just listen for three years. Whether you understand or not, just sit in front of me and listen to what I say. Don't be impatient and say you're going to give up study and return to your village. Just give me three years. Just sit in front of me for three years—you don't have to pay attention—and let me talk.

Buddhism isn't a matter of knowledge. It is something communicated from one person to another. The important information seeps into you through the pores of your skin. Although you may not understand, just sit still and listen. I want to believe that the young monk decided to try attending Saeki's lectures once again and, at the very least, sat there silently listening to Saeki's voice for three years.

The School of the Ear

I write of many things here as if I knew them, but in fact most of my knowledge and understanding of this subject comes not from texts but from what is called "the school of the ear," from listening to what others have told me.

Aren't true knowledge and understanding things that must be spoken aloud, passed from the mouth of a speaker to the ear of a listener?

The story I have just related tells us that logic and reasoning are not the only important things when studying Buddhism. It is also very important that the teacher's soul, his passion, his sincerity, are communicated. There is much talk today about the renewed importance of religion and the need to revive religious faith, but we can only achieve this if we encounter a person who we are willing to follow, without regrets. To put it another way, we can only find religion if we encounter someone who can impart feeling-filled information (*joho*) to us, and if we have the flexibility of mind and spirit to receive and accept that *joho*.

It is not simply a matter of intellectually understanding every single detailed point and argument. The True Pure Land sect has always placed special value on oral teachings. Rennyo's well-known *Gobunsho* (also called *Ofumi,* or Letters) are sermons in the form of letters that were written to be read aloud to a large group, or for the group to actually recite in unison. Saeki lectured to people at Horyuji as an expression of his sincere wish to teach the Dharma, the philosophy of Buddhism, to others. Even though the students might not understand all the intricacies of doctrine, if they sat in front of him for three years, listening to what he had to say, his overflowing passion for his subject, his feeling, would be communicated by his voice and his expression and would seep into their very beings. That is what is most important, after all.

This, I believe, is the meaning of *menju.*

Books are fine for abstract intellectual learning. But there are some things we cannot get from books. We must recognize the importance of learning by sitting face-to-face and hearing a person's voice, touching his hand, having physical contact. There are also important things the nonverbal communication of the voice and the face can offer that reasoning cannot. We can feel these nonverbal messages. We don't only understand them, we feel them. This episode about Join Saeki reminds us that these nonverbal messages are also very important to us.

On the other hand, there are times when one can experience something like *menju* through the medium of the written word as well. Several years ago I decided to read Hyakuzo Kurata's *Shukke* to *Sono Deshi* (The monk and his disciple). I was writing a play myself, and I was embarrassed not to have read such a masterpiece as Kurata's play, so I decided to put an end to my ignorance.

True Sadness Comes Someday

One part of the play that struck me in particular was a conversation between the monk—Shinran, the play's leading character—and his disciple, the young monk Yuien. Yuien is believed to be the compiler of the *Tannisho* (Lamenting heresy), a collection of Shinran's remarks on various subjects. There is a scene in which Shinran and Yuien are looking outside and conversing. When I read this scene, I visualized it as clearly as a scene in a film. Yuien, gazing outside, says softly to Shinran, "Master, I have been feeling so sad lately. Sometimes, even just watching people walking down the street, I am overcome by a feeling of sadness and I start to weep. Is there something wrong with me?"

Shinran replies, "There's nothing wrong with you. You're fine,

Yuien, just fine. If you feel sad, feel sad. There's nothing you can do about it." Yuien asks again, "Does even a person such as yourself, master, feel sad at times?"

Does even someone of such firm faith, such a great man, experience sadness? In response, Shinran replies, "I am sad, too. But, Yuien, the sadness you are feeling now and my sadness are a bit different. Your sadness will pass with time. It is a sadness that can be cured, but the sadness I feel is a profound, weighty sadness that has sunk deep into my very bones. And I know that I will carry this sadness with me for the rest of my life."

So Shinran speaks, not as a master to a disciple, but as a man speaking to his young friend. Shinran goes on to say, "The time will come when you can understand this true sadness I speak of, when you will come to feel it yourself. Yuien, when that time comes, do not try to escape from that sadness or ignore it or pretend you don't feel it. Do not deceive yourself, but look right into it and follow your heart. That true sadness is your fate, trying to teach you something."

It seems to me that Kurata has Shinran saying that true faith, although it can certainly be found within the extreme circumstances of harsh ascetic practice, is not found only there. True faith can also sprout when a person is crushed under the weight of tremendous sadness. In other words, all human experiences can be doors to what it is that we seek. We should accept our experiences openly, and face them head-on. This is what I think Kurata has Shinran saying in his play.

We read what the writer Hyakuzo Kurata has written, and we experience the same feeling as the character Yuien does, who is receiving this "direct transmission" (*menju*) from his master. We feel as if Shinran were actually talking to us like a friend.

Although the words of the play are in written form, we experience the illusion of hearing Shinran's living voice in them. This is one of the extremely strange and wonderful powers of language, of books, of the printed word.

There are words that even in written form seem alive and can change one's innermost feelings. At the same time, this has its limits.

Religious ideas and faith, in particular, cannot be fully transmitted through books or by philosophical argument. They must be imparted within the context of human relationships, directly from one human being to another, in an interlinked chain. In direct transmission, we can communicate not just with words but with our breathing, the glow of the skin, the color of the eyes. Both means of communication are extremely important.

Hope, for example, shines more brightly in the pit of despair. If all were light and brightness, we would have a difficult time recognizing hope. We must be in a state of despair, of sadness, of confusion, or of pain for our minds to begin to reach out to try to grasp a way out. In the process of moving back and forth between these opposites, hope and despair, we come to understand life. The trigger may be spoken words or written words, or it may be direct transmission.

Today people meet, shop, talk, and work together over the telephone and the Internet. I have no intention of rejecting such innovations. The books we read were, at one time, also a great media revolution.

These new media are an extension of books and writing, and I think they are fine in their place, but as computers come to play a larger part in education and our lives, I think we also need to place greater importance on direct interaction among people—direct transmission—and unless we do so we will be losing something very important to us all.

VI. Living with Illness

We Are All Ill

Western philosophy seeks to deny or reject illness. According to it, the ideal human condition is one free of disease.

This is the basis for modern medicine and medical treatment.

Since modern medical treatment has prevailed for so long, the automatic response to the discovery of disease is to seek to eliminate it. Modern medicine cannot conceive of an approach that tries to find a way to live with one's illness, embracing it and accepting it.

The dawn of modern Western medicine predates the French Revolution by a few years, with the founding of the Hospital in Paris. Dedicated young doctors gathered there to practice their ideal conception of medicine, based on the spirit of liberty, equality, and fraternity. They diagnosed and treated the common people. Up until that time, medical treatment had largely been the work of personal physicians attached to wealthy patrons, and these young doctors strove to break away from that tradition.

The motto of the doctors at the hospital was "Look at the disease, not the patient."

By "looking at the disease," they meant employing statistical public health information to scientifically analyze and categorize the symptoms. "Not looking at the patient" meant paying no attention to the person's social status or class, but treating his sickness as one would any other patient in the same condition.

These young doctors burned with a passion to eliminate disease entirely.

But after two centuries, their approach evolved into a way of thinking represented by the old chestnut "The surgery was a success, but the patient died." Modern medicine focuses solely on disease and ignores the individual's background and quality of life. It sees a person as a thing that must be poked and prodded until it is reduced to digital data. It depends too heavily on drugs. It has no regard for the individual's human dignity or emotions.

Yet, the modern medical approach is not universal. In Zen, they call sickness a "disturbance" (*fuan*), and believe that there are 404 illnesses waiting to surface from inside the body. When they say, "The Roshi is disturbed," it means he's ill. "Disturbed" here means that the body has become upset and imbalanced, and that one of the 404 illnesses has asserted itself. Buddhist belief requires that we live in harmony with our illnesses.

Western medicine is part and parcel of Western culture and civilization, and Western civilization, because of its enormous economic and military force, has had a dominant impact on the entire world. But there are many differing concepts of the human body and health, and even Western medicine has begun to reexamine the question of why illness occurs.

Now is the time for us to fundamentally rethink our ideas about disease and health.

We are all ill. All human beings are sick, and health is an illusion. Every day our teeth grow weaker, our skin ages, and more than 100,000 brain cells die, never to be replaced. All the cells of our body are constantly disintegrating and dying and being replaced by others.

It is impossible for a monolithic, static, and dogmatic model of health care to meet the needs of such a constantly changing, dynamic, living being.

Each of us is completely different.

For that reason, medicine must treat each of us as the individuals we are, considering such things as our philosophical beliefs, our family situations, and our personal problems, and decide, based on that totality, whether or not to prescribe medicine or to advise surgery. Our doctors can decide nothing for us, but they can help us see what our choices are and help us decide what is best for our lives.

What is needed now is the Buddhist concept of living with illness.

Quality of Death

It is rare for death to be such a frequently discussed topic as it is today. There was a period when life was a popular theme for discussion, but lately more attention has been directed at death. We even have the term "quality of death."

My mother and father died young. Only two of their five children survive. No doubt it has something to do with the fact that I grew up during wartime, but from my teens I was aware of death as something that comes suddenly.

Although I am not aloof to my own death, of course, I have suffered greatly and endured much in my life, and I hope I can meet death with a feeling of calm and peace: "I'm tired, and it's time to rest." Since we have no choice or freedom in our birth, I have always thought that I would like to choose the time of my death. Being upset by death is a choice, just as letting nature take its course is a choice. I would prefer to meet death without much fuss.

Let's talk about cancer. We look at cancer as something that harms the body and must be eliminated, but on the level of molecular biology, there are new theories that describe an alternate way of viewing cancer. The director of the Sapporo Cancer Seminar and leading cancer pathologist Dr. Hiroshi Kobayashi has written that there are fifty trillion cells in our bodies, and all of them are aging. They are also being constantly harmed by ultraviolet radiation, pollutants, and other toxins. According to Kobayashi, cancer originates in the body's effort to somehow assist and sustain those damaged and aging cells.

All living things are made up of cells, and life is supported by the constant renewal of those cells through division as older cells die and disappear. When cells are aging or damaged and losing the power to divide and reproduce, volunteer cells gather around them to "back them up." They do their best to "cover" for the less vigorous cells by dividing and reproducing very actively. Then something goes wrong, and they cannot stop themselves. They are unable to stop reproducing, run wild, and replicate uncontrollably. This is cancer.

Two features can be identified in the appearance of a cancer. First, it reproduces at an uncontrollable rate, like a car speeding forward when the accelerator is stuck to the floor. The second feature is that the normal control mechanism for reproduction ceases to function. In other words, the brakes fail.

Nevertheless, cancer first appears with good intentions. In that sense, the way of thinking that leads to trying to destroy the cancer cells or burn them with radiation, the concept of fighting them, is flawed.

If a family member is crying for help as he runs out of control, the family must somehow pull together to help him. In the same way, it is one's own cells that have become cancerous and are causing harm to the body, so one must somehow bring them back from the brink. What is needed is the power to control their runaway reproduction, a way to slow them down. I am talking about a treatment that does not destroy the cancer but "rescues" it from itself.

Sympathetic Treatment and Antagonistic Treatment

I just happened to come across an essay by Dr. Masaru Komazawa in a 1983 edition of *Nihon Iji Shimpo* (New journal of Japanese medicine) entitled "Medicine, Me, and Shinran."

In the essay, Dr. Komazawa looks at the very foundation of the science of medicine from the perspective of Buddhism. Part of the essay in particular made a deep impression on me, and I would like to paraphrase it here.

Medicine naturally seeks health as its goal. But in doing so, suggests Komazawa, perhaps it is misguided. Does health really equal happiness? Aren't there cases in which health and a person's spiritual happiness are not identical? Medicine always and unconditionally pursues health, and that reveals its profound misunderstanding of the human condition. This is Dr. Komazawa's opinion, and in the article he explores the question of human happiness from another perspective, while retaining his stance as a doctor.

In his essay, Dr. Komazawa introduces and summarizes a case published in *The New England Journal of Medicine.** A forty-four-year-old woman became pregnant with twins. Amniocentesis revealed that one of the twins was normal, while the other had Down's syndrome. The mother asked the doctor to kill the embryo afflicted with Down's syndrome and allow her to give birth only to

*Kerenyi, Thomas D. and Usha Chitkara, "Selective Birth in Twin Pregnancy with Dscordancy for Down's Syndrome," *The New England Journal of Medicine* 304 (June 18, 1981): 1525–27.

the healthy child. I can't say that I don't understand the mother's feelings. Knowing that a child will be born with a severe handicap and will suffer much in life must have been very painful for her. But it is what happened next that is important.

Responding to the mother's wish, her doctor employed the latest knowledge and technology to kill the afflicted child without adversely affecting the mother or the normal twin.

The article in *The New England Journal of Medicine* described the methods and procedures employed. Before starting, the doctors first acquired permission from the courts, then coolly and scientifically went about their task.

First the exact position and location of the embryo was determined through ultrasound. The heart of the embryo with Down's syndrome was identified, and a large needle inserted into the womb. The first attempt failed, and the needle did not puncture the heart. The second attempt was a success. Once the needle had punctured the embryo's heart, it was used to gradually drain it of blood.

This was an application of the newest surgical techniques to prevent the birth of a handicapped child. The entire procedure was monitored objectively and scientifically. The condition of the heart of the other, healthy twin and other factors were all carefully observed.

Eventually, after twenty cubic centimeters of blood were withdrawn from the embryo's heart, it stopped beating.

The subsequent treatment of the mother and the remaining twin went smoothly, and later she gave birth to a healthy child.

Dr. Komazawa says that after reading this report in *The New England Journal of Medicine,* he was very disturbed.

Why did Dr. Komazawa react the way he did? This is how he explains it. "The reason I was so disturbed was because I was not entirely opposed to the motivation for or the method adopted to kill the twin. In other words, I couldn't put my finger on what was wrong about it."

How would I react if I were to learn that my unborn child had Down's syndrome? Especially in a case such as this, with twins, and one of them healthy?

When I think about what I would do, I admit that I don't have a clear answer. And I can only begin to imagine how a mother would feel in that situation. I would probably arrive at the same decision as the mother in the article. After much long, hard, and painful thought.

Let us return to the question of why Dr. Komazawa, who had read a great deal about the medical treatment of Down's syndrome, was so disturbed.

"When I think of the mother's earnest wish not to give birth to a child suffering from Down's syndrome, I can't regard the steps taken as wrong. The medical procedures employed are not outside of the purview of normal medicine. I was disturbed because the thinking behind this medical procedure was essentially the same as that behind our treatment of pneumonia, for example, or our attempts to find a cure for infant cancer."

Then Dr. Komazawa reflected and asked himself, "Is my medical treatment misguided, too?"

What is this "misguided"? The essence of this misguidedness is that "medicine is based on negation of the human condition."

Komazawa wrote, "Medicine is based on negation, on rejection. For example, medicine says that there's something wrong with a person who can't see, a person who can't hear, a person who can't use all four limbs freely, and so forth. This negation and rejection are the starting point of all medicine."

This seems completely natural to us. There's nothing particularly frightening about the fact that medicine begins by rejecting disease, is there? The entire modern age is defined by its rejection of all that came before it, after all.

Here Dr. Komazawa is reminded of a published discussion between Yonezo Nakagawa and Benzaburo Kato that he once read. "In that discussion, Kato talked about sympathetic treatment (*doji*) and antagonistic treatment (*taiji*). These are Buddhist terms. An example of antagonistic treatment is to use ice to bring down a fever, while sympathetic treatment for the same fever is to wrap the patient in blankets and make him sweat. Antagonistic treatment of a person who is grieving is to say, 'There's no use being sad, perk up!'; sympathetic treatment is to sit down and share a good cry with the grieving person and thus help him put down his burden of sadness. Kato went on to say that in many situations sympathetic treatment was usually more effective."

This is the first time I had heard of antagonistic and sympathetic treatment, and I was struck by what an interesting concept this is. The same seems to have been true for Dr. Komazawa, but he also says that for some time he didn't really grasp the meaning of sympathetic treatment.

He says that he had interpreted sympathetic treatment as putting oneself in the patient's shoes and treating him with kindness. But that is not actually it. He says he realized this when he was involved in treating a child who was anorexic.

"After the child was hospitalized, the head doctor did everything he could. He investigated every possibility he could think of— whether there was a problem in the child's relationship with his parents, or with school, or where he lived. He looked on the child with a parent's eyes, and he did everything in his power to encourage him to eat."

It was at this point that Dr. Komazawa realized that although everyone in contact with the child was treating him kindly, this was not really sympathetic treatment.

"In other words, the efforts of all those around him were concentrated on telling the child that he was not permitted to not eat. They were opposing the child's behavior. They may have been trying to be kind to him, but they were treating him antagonistically, their approach started from rejection. . . . No matter how kindly it may be, all medical treatment is antagonistic, in other words, negative, and sympathetic treatment is impossible within the confines of modern medicine."

Antagonist treatment is a philosophy of subjugation and control. This is why modern medicine and science are misguided, says Dr. Komazawa.

"The attitude of accepting death, of affirming it, is sympathetic treatment. Urging a dying person to live is the same as urging a living person to die. Isn't the true friend the one who tells a dying person that it's all right to die?"

No one can deny death. Yet, modern medicine, in its attempts to prolong life, continues to deny death and treat it as an absolute evil. I have lost many people who were very close to me. I know very well, to an unpleasant degree, how hard it is to say to a dying person, "All right, you don't have to keep fighting anymore. It was hard, I know. You can go now, you can go."

Dr. Komazawa introduces another episode, which is based on the journal of the mother of a young girl who was dying of leukemia:

When there were no more medicines that would stop the leukemia, the mother brought her child home. She made an effort to make the time she spent at home pleasant. At home, life was freer than in the hospital, and the girl could eat and take a bath whenever she pleased.

At home, if she was feeling bad at night, the mother would take her outside and they would look at the stars together. If she was feeling well during the day, her father would give her a ride on his tractor, which she loved.

But finally the little girl's last day came, and she lay still, gasping for breath. To her mother, the gasps seemed exactly like the labor pains she had experienced when she was giving birth to her child. The mother cheered her daughter on in death. When she finally died, the mother thought, just as when she had been born, "Hurray! She did it! My little girl has won over death!"

We cannot help but be shocked by the feeling of this mother, praying for the successful death of her child.

We can easily say, "Live!" but as long as we think of death as bad and affirm only life, it would never occur to us to cheer someone on in death. Reading Dr. Komazawa's essay, I couldn't help but be newly struck by the fundamental problem of modern thought, which divides existence into good and evil and rejects one or the other of the two extremes. Should we reject old age? Is illness an absolute evil? Why do we fear death? As long as we retain our present attitudes, the path ahead remains dark. What we need now is a worldview that affirms all of reality—sympathetic treatment. That was my reaction as I read Dr. Komazawa's essay.

Flowing Down

There are two kinds of Buddhas in Japan. One is called in Japanese *nyorai* (Thus-Come One) and the other, *nyoko* (Thus-Gone One).

"Thus" refers to "thusness," a Buddhist term for true reality just as it is. The Thus-Gone One is the solitary figure who approaches truth one step at a time. He is respected by all, who bow to his receding figure and try to follow in his footsteps. The Thus-Come One, on the other hand, is the Buddha who comes to our world from the realm of absolute truth. While the Thus-Gone One leads with his back to us, the Thus-Come One saves all beings, so he must face us. In an act of supreme service, he offers his hand to us, embracing even those who do not hearken to him, calling out to them to look his way. This is the Thus-Come One.

Shinran calls these two aspects of the Buddha *ogen,* or "going and returning."

Throughout my life, I have always thought that flowing down, like water, is a good thing. Rain falls on the forest, dripping from the trees' leaves down into the soil, where it forms rivulets and streams. These flow down, down, pure and dirty water alike joining into rivers that flow into the sea. When I think of myself as a single drop of water in the flow of that mighty river, I am one of the many things flowing down toward the depths.

We have the words "lowly" and "lofty," and we tend to think that high means good and low means bad. We also tend to think of "dry" humor as being sophisticated and "wet" emotions as being vulgar and sentimental.

The modern sensibility has firmly rejected the emotional. But isn't it the parched and dry spirit that is the cause of so much of the premeditated cruelty that has marked this century?

Genuine Positive Thinking Derives from Radically Negative Thinking

We have no control over our birth, and we cannot avoid aging. We all fall ill. And we must all face death, without exception. Human existence is defined by these four facts, and we cannot change them by our acts or force of will. Gautama realized that these were the common fate of all humanity, no matter how far civilization advanced, no matter how the times changed, and no matter what the people or culture.

Accepting this reality, is it then possible for a human being, defined by these four inevitabilities, to live a life filled with vitality and hope?

The young man who was later known as the Buddha set out on the spiritual quest to answer this question at the age of twenty-nine. He abandoned his family and his life of ease to do so.

Starting from this radically negative way of thinking, he finally came to affirm human existence, and from that day forward he was known as the Buddha—the enlightened one.

I believe that the reason the Buddha's words make such a strong impression on us today is because he was able to arrive at a firmly established positive way of thinking from his original radically negative position.

What has usually been regarded as "positive thinking" up to now is really little more than mindless optimism, a vague feeling of hope; it is not something that can be a true source of strength in life. Genuine positive thinking is something else altogether.

What is it? Consider the fate of a man who has seen endless suffering in his life, who has watched his family, his countrymen, his traditions, and all he holds sacred, tortured, abused, and destroyed. Yet, his aspect toward life is wholly compassionate, warm, even joyful. Is he a fool? Has he gone mad? Not at all. He is enlightened. He is not ruled by fear that his comfortable life will be overturned for he has already survived such upheaval, even though nothing will ever redeem his endless sorrow. This is the story of the Dalai Lama.

After the Buddha left his father's palace, he could think of nothing but illness, age, and death. He brought suffering upon himself because he could not live in sheltered ignorance of it, the knowledge alone was too unbearable. After eight years of starving himself of food and human companionship, he achieved his enlightenment. Enlightenment accompanied his embrace of the intransigent and central fact of human suffering. He returned to the world to carry on his work and spread his teachings.

The first thing we must do, right now, is to face reality, to look directly at the enormous threat to the human spirit. The question we must answer is not "What is humanity?" but "What are we to do now, given what we know?"

Once one accepts the inevitability of suffering, the omnipresence of death, what is there to fear in life?

One must have the courage to lose things, or to give up things. Only then can we be truly free. Only then can we see life for what it really is.

Looking Down from the Mountaintop

Since ancient times, it has been a common understanding in India that life is divided into four stages or passages. The first stage was the life of a student, a period of study and preparation before one enters society. In modern terms, this corresponds to the period of life up to about the mid-twenties.

The second stage was that of the householder. During this period, one had a family and made a contribution to society. This is equivalent today to the period of our lives up to retirement. After completing the householder's duties and responsibilities, one entered a period of seclusion and contemplation. One became a "forest dweller." During this time one lives alone in the midst of nature, thinking about one's life and the nature of the human experience. Separated from the rush of life, one enters into a dialogue with the self, and looks long and hard at one's existence as a tiny part of the vast cosmos.

When does the time come to withdraw from the front lines of

life? The idea of living in the forest calls to mind the famous Japanese work *Hojoki* (Tales of a ten-foot-square hut) by Kamo no Chomei (1155–1216). Chomei left the capital, Kyoto, and built a rough hut to live in when he was fifty. Nowadays, the period of the householder is considerably longer, particularly in the West, where people often work well after retirement age. In general, however, the period of the forest dweller may be said to begin when the children have all been married off and settled into their own householder lives. After this, whatever age one is, one should begin to live a more human, self-reflective life following the natural rhythms of work and relaxation. It is important to leave enough time for this period of one's life.

After passing through the period of the forest dweller, as one senses the approach of life's end, one enters the period of the wandering hermit. This is a time of pilgrimage. One travels to the shores of the sacred river and awaits death. One abandons one's home and wealth and departs on the journey with only a single pilgrim's robe. It is, I think, a journey to death.

I bring up this ancient Indian view of life because I think that we are living in a time in which we have lost sight of our own future. In Japan we saw ourselves soaring through a period of high economic growth with the fear of the past, the fear of the deprivation we had so recently escaped, preventing us from looking back. The West is now riding up that ascent at full tilt, without a backward glance.

In mountain climbing, reaching the peak is not the end. One must also safely descend again. One might think that there's nothing to descending, but in fact it requires even greater concentration and skill than the ascent does.

We are seeing a need, in various realms of human activity, for the wisdom to apply the brakes and slow things down.

If we compare a society's fate with an individual human life, using the Chinese system of the four seasons, America, like Japan, cannot remain forever in the green spring of youth, nor does it seem to be in the red heat of summer any longer. That means we are heading for the white autumn. This is not simply a season of declining energies. It is a time of reining in rampant, wild energies, achieving a state of calm, and building a mature, ripe culture.

Today we are sitting on the mountaintop. We have crossed the summit. We must think carefully about how to enjoy a beautiful descent, a fulfilling and fruitful descent, down from the heights to lowlands on the other side.

VII. Flexibility Is Life

A Lack of Imagination

We perceive ourselves as existing in a continuum of time running from past to future, and we also recognize a social continuum in which we exist.

Stories form the warp and weft of these continuums, they create a web of meaning that is carried from one life to the next, from one period of history to the next. When we lose our story, we can no longer retain our place in those continuums.

Children's lives used to be filled with stories their parents and grandparents passed down to them; these were the stories that filled their imaginations, their dreams, their sense of themselves. These were the books that sustained them, year after year, generation after generation. That is no longer true today.

Today the storyteller is the television set and the computer game. The characters are often one-dimensional: "good" and "evil." There is little that is emotionally sustaining in the plots they weave, and when the endings are predictable, children do not learn the complexities of real life, the disappointments, the imperfections, the pathos, the poignant joys. There is an emptiness in the violence of these new media, a visual effect rather than an emotional maturity. When a child who is filled with more human stories pulls out a knife, he will be able to imagine, in a flash, the consequences of using that knife. His imaginative powers will tell him what will happen next based on what he has learned from the stories he has been told, the books he has read, the cautionary tales of his parents and elders. When a child who has been reared by a television set pulls out a knife, he is more likely to want to watch what happens, feeling himself a passive spectator, rather than to consider and reflect on the consequences of actions he can barely discern are his own. The results of this kind of indoctrination are all around us. The unspeakable and empty violence of our children, children raised in a relatively peaceful historical moment, is all around us.

When people lose the ability to imagine what will happen next, they have lost the thread of their own story and the stories of others. They have stepped out of the continuum that sustains them.

Imagination is at the root of a story, and our existence is supported by our stories.

The Buddha embarked on a search for a way to live life fully and vibrantly, in spite of the omnipresence of birth, old age, sickness, and death. And by the time of his death he had found such a way, and had radically affirmed life and the world for all those who would follow him. His story has affected all of our lives. He helps us imagine a way to be happy, without disowning our sufferings.

If we can perceive our lives as nothing more than a small part of the larger flow of being, we may, while disgusted with our own foolishness and pettiness, also be able to feel a great abiding love for existence itself.

That is when we find our place in the continuum, and it is from there that the potential to create our story arises.

Flexibility Is Life

Shinran experienced his religious conversion in the form of a dream in which Prince Shotoku appeared to him with a message. In those days, sleep and dreams were considered important enough to actually transform a person's life. With our rushing madly about during our every waking hour, we have cut ourselves off from this dream life and the special kind of wisdom it brings to our notice, if we let it. Daydreaming, meditation, and simple rest and relaxation can reset our minds, opening them to all kinds of new experiences and revelations.

The great Taoist philosopher Lao-tsu insisted upon the importance of flexibility, of softness, pointing out that we are most flexible and soft as children, grow stiff as we age, and become completely rigid when we die.

Flexibility is life: That's how important it is.

But our values and attitudes today do not see the virtues of flexibility. We see only one aspect of life, we are overly focused on achieving our professional goals, on asserting our will and control over the terms of our existence. Anything that serves to interrupt our focus, to disrupt the stream of tasks we set out to accomplish every day, is considered unwelcome.

Consider the man who neglects his wife and children so that he can concentrate utterly on the work he must do to support them. When his wife grows distant and his children become strangers, he only tells himself that without his job, they wouldn't have the nice house to live in, the after-school treats. When his wife asks instead for emotional sustenance, he withdraws fearfully, considering the fulfillment of such needs a sign of weakness.

The Japanese word *joho* is often translated as "information," but it does not in fact refer to cold, objective numerical data. *Jo,* the first character in *joho,* means "feeling." Feelings are also facts. Feelings are also information, though not the sort that can be sorted and counted. Genuine knowledge, genuine *joho,* must contain emotion, it must express grief or anger or happiness or hope.

Genuine *joho* is by nature personal and intimate, something communicated from one person to another.

A Person of Great Sympathy

The Japanese word *jihi,* often translated as "compassion," is actually made up of two parts, *ji* and *hi*. *Ji* is a translation of the Pali word *maitri,* while *hi* is the translation of the Sanskrit *karuna,* which means "a sigh." To use a musical metaphor, *ji* is a major chord and *hi* is a minor chord.

A certain father, an important businessman, went to great lengths to free his son from a religious cult. He quit his job, and then he read all of the books on religion on his son's bookshelf. Every day he argued with his son about religion, doing his best to persuade him to quit the cult. The father told his son that by recognizing and making amends for his mistake he could start anew, and he encouraged his son to accept his help so that they could, together, build a better life. This is *ji,* the major chord. This attitude toward his son of positive, compassionate engagement represents *ji* or *maitri*.

On the other hand, his mother said nothing but sat beside her husband weeping softly as the endless religious debates went on. We can describe her attitude of silent sympathy as *hi* or *karuna*. *Hi* is the sympathetic identification with another's sufferings, even though you can do nothing to actually relieve the suffering. You cannot take another's pain on yourself.

His mother did not ask him why he had joined the cult, or any other questions; she simply placed her hand over that of her child, accepting his pain as her own, letting him know that whatever might happen to him, she would stand by him.

This is the embodiment of *hi,* the minor chord.

There are times when people can be comforted only by such *hi,* by this minor chord.

Up to now, there has been relatively little interest in our society in the feeling of *hi,* at least compared to *ji.*

Sitting silently, letting the tears fall, sighing in sympathy—you may think this is of no use to the person who is suffering, but there are times when it is a tremendous help.

The novelist Shusaku Endo (1923–98) once wrote, "The mental pain and suffering of the sick person, the person struggling with a problem, cannot be communicated to others. When he thinks that he alone feels this pain, it seems twice or three times as great." When we keep grief and suffering inside, they become a burden twice or three times heavier than they actually are.

Such utterly personal and interior grief and suffering cannot be healed by encouraging words. What can you do at such a time? Just sit quietly beside the person in pain. Take his hand in yours, and weep with him. That's enough. Sigh a deep sigh. With the spread of the warmth of your hand into his, his hidden grief and pain will be communicated to you and dispersed.

Let us imagine a son who is sentenced to prison.

A father filled with compassion may encourage his son, "Don't give up hope! Pay for your crime and come back to us and make a new start. We will be here waiting for you. We'll join hands and begin on a new future together."

But what does his mother do? She does not press him with questions such as "How did this happen? What are you going to do?" She just sits silently by her son's side, weeping and looking into his face.

She takes his hand in hers, her head bowed, her whole being saying: "Even if you were to fall into hell, I would go with you."

This message is the one that reaches deepest into the heart. It is the only thing that can save a person who has given up. This is *hi*.

Suicide and Murder Are Two Sides of the Same Coin

Suicide is a light step over to the side of death to escape the pain of being alive. This is an easy thing to do if you lack a strong sense of the value of your life, the preciousness of your existence as an individual.

Perhaps another way to describe this lack of a sense of your life's rarity and worth is to say that *one feels invisible*.

The inability to feel the weight of one's existence is surely a characteristic of our times. And the inability to appreciate the value of one's own life means that one cannot appreciate the value of others' lives, either.

Suicide and murder are not just separated by a thin line. They are more intimately connected: They are two sides of the same coin. People frequently remark with a sigh that violent crimes seem to be on the rise these days, and this is not unrelated to the rise in suicides. In fact, they are directly related.

We are living in a time when we are all just as close to death as we were during the war, a time when people think little of stepping over the line that separates life from death themselves, and just as little as pushing others over that line. We call this peace, but perhaps this is no more than a vain daydream, an illusion of peace.

Let us imagine that your greatest fear is to become hopelessly in debt with no way to find your way out, except by suicide. You foresee bankruptcy and the shame that will follow it. You will lose the faith and trust of your family and community. Your family may be destroyed in the process. But even if your wife divorces you, even if you must leave your home, all this will serve to deepen your spirit and your grasp of the meaning of life.

It is an opportunity for a great teaching that perhaps could have come to you in no other way. You must continue living to understand it.

There is an old Buddhist term, *ocho,* which means overcoming by going around. In confronting a problem or crisis head-on, you may encounter a wall so high and thick that you cannot break through it. So you turn to one side and go around the wall. This is *ocho.* Instead of sitting desolately in front of the wall that is blocking your progress, you try to get around it by making a long detour, or even by digging under it. Suddenly your despair is transformed into an obstacle, something that can be grappled with, something that can be broken down, clambered over, outsmarted. It is a subtle but simple movement of the mind that makes this transformation complete, but an invaluable one to learn and perfect.

Let me tell you the story of a woman who was very depressed because she was alone. Despite professional success, she felt that she was a failure in the eyes of her family because she had not found a man to marry and to have children with. She worried she would become bitter and angry as she grew older. Her relationships with her family began to suffer. She felt they were all waiting for the same thing she was waiting for. She worked all the time and avoided her friends because she did not want to bore them with her sad story. Day after day she sat in front of her wall and contemplated it morosely. Then, one day, she looked up. The sun was shining. She picked up the phone and called a friend who was happy to hear from her. They had dinner together. Hours passed and she realized that she was still alone. Yet, her journey had changed.

I hope that people who are so driven to desperation that they are considering death will remember the tried-and-true Buddhist tactic of *ocho*.

We Are All Alone

After the Kobe earthquake struck, killing thousands and making thousands more homeless, people were in shock and searching for meaning. And just as people were starting to recover from the shock of that, the Aum Shinrikyo religious cult released nerve gas in the Tokyo subway, killing and harming many innocent passengers. So just as the material world can be deadly, the spiritual world provides no easy refuge.

A simple way of saying this is that the external world cannot be counted on, and we have no alternative but to rely on the inner world, the self. This irreplaceable individual, this unique self, lives alone and isolated in an illusory, empty world.

We may take our life in one direction or the other, we may choose the mountains or the sea, but wherever we may go, we must live that life. When we then ask ourselves just what this self is, we find only a small, fragile thing consisting of an unreliable little body and an easily wounded heart.

I once met an Israeli theater director whose company was performing *Hamlet* in Japan. He said that Hamlet's famous question, "To be or not to be," was a question for our time, and I disagreed. "The person who can ask whether he should or should not be is very fortunate," I said. "In Africa and many other places all around the world, millions of people are just desperately trying to survive today and tomorrow. They are not thinking about whether or not they should exist but how. This situation, in my opinion, is the true question of our time."

But as we look at our world, we see strife and conflict everywhere and mass environmental destruction. Although we are on the verge of entering a new age, our world is at the same time in the last stages of a fatal illness. Faced with such circumstances, we are asking ourselves anew how we should live.

How hard it is to live this life, even if we accomplish nothing in it. How grateful, then, we should be to those who have achieved great things. We need not be embarrassed that we cannot be like them, because just living is hard enough. People should be praised simply for surviving fifty or sixty years. Certainly, no matter what kind of life a person has had, he or she has done the best possible.

You may feel that you are nothing to be proud of, but why not simply accept who you are? Just as good and evil coexist within us, two modes of living—to live well and simply to exist—also coexist, wrapped around each other like a double helix. It is wrong to conclude that if one cannot live a fully realized human life one doesn't have a right to exist at all. I believe that humans have an instinctual force that leads them in the direction of trying to live as fully human a life as possible.

But the first step for this lonely, isolated being in an empty world is simply to exist.

The Deeper One Feels Grief, the Stronger One Feels Joy

In order to live your life as an independent individual, you must first arouse various capacities within yourself.

One of these capacities is the five senses. Traditionally, the Japanese have placed a high value on the five senses. The sense of touch is a good example: Being pleasant to the touch was a highly valued quality in the utensils of daily life and in clothing.

Today we no longer pay much attention to this quality.

There is so much plastic, glass, and metal in our lives that our sensitivity to touch has declined drastically. It also seems that the number of young people with dulled senses of taste and smell is increasing. I think it's fair to say that the sensitivity of the five senses that all humans are born with has reached its lowest limit.

Just as important as refining our five senses is the need to feel deeply, to know strong joy and deep sorrow.

People should laugh loudly and weep profusely. The deeper the grief you feel, the stronger the joy you can feel. The more a person cries, the more he can laugh.

There are times when a person drops to the deepest depths of melancholy and despair, but this is an important part of the human spirit.

Up to now, the ideal employee was said to be a go-getter. A go-getter was someone who strived at all costs to prevail not only at work but in his private life as well. Such individuals are relentlessly positive and utterly refuse to accept even the possibility of failure. They are strongly goal oriented, and if they fail to achieve their goals for some reason, they regard themselves as failures as human beings, ending up in the state of self-hate, despair, and neurosis that they sought so hard to avoid.

We mustn't think of emotions as hindrances or failings. Developing a broad-ranging emotional compass that allows us to live freely and vigorously is not only a plus in daily life but will also reward us with a high degree of respect and trust in our social lives.

We Are All Born Crying

"Is there really anything we can hope for from life?" I have asked myself this question since I was young, and I have never fully answered it. Most people don't think about this very much, but for some reason whenever I am deeply depressed this thought occurs to me.

We tend to try to avoid this question.

But try as we might to avoid it or shut our eyes to it, there comes a time when we must ask it in earnest, and the earlier the better. I think it is much better to live with this question from your youth than to suddenly awaken to it after you have become old.

The reason? Because, in my opinion at least, there are no ready-made hopes in life.

I have often repeated these memorable words from Shakespeare's *King Lear* in my writings: "When we are born, we cry that we are come / To this great stage of fools."*

Three undeniable truths are encapsulated in these lines.

First, we cannot determine our birth. We do not have the power to decide when we will be born, in what country, in whose home, into which ethnic group, nor the profession of our family, what kind of physical or mental traits we will have, our personality, or our genetic make-up. From the very first step, our lives are determined by some other power, which is out of our control and unaffected by our efforts or will.

The second truth is that each of us is on a journey that, day by day, approaches death. Our future offers us one choice and one choice alone: death. Human life is a sad and futile thing, moving a step nearer to death each day.

King Lear, Act IV, sc.vi,ls. 185–86.

Finally, life has limits. It is rare to live to be over one hundred years old. However rich or powerful you may be, you will never have immortality.

When these three truths rise up before your eyes, you feel helpless, you grasp the futility of life, become dispirited, and sink into deep thought. In the nineteenth century, they used to call this state "melancholy."

"There Is Nothing I Can Do"

I am like a person from a tribe of itinerant wanderers, with little interest in a permanent home. I feel strongly that any proof of the fact that I lived, any trace, will be blown away in the wind, and no sign of my existence will remain. I don't even know how many books I have written, and I have never kept any of my manuscripts. This may be a symptom of my childhood experience of having all that I knew taken from me as we retreated, leaving everything behind, after the end of the war.

When people ask me what I believe in, I hear a soft whisper from the depths of my heart: "There is nothing I can do."

For many years I have practiced a sort of "death exercise." Each night I perform a ritual.

Before I go to sleep, I breathe deeply and ask myself whether I would be satisfied if I didn't open my eyes the next morning. If I were not to awake the next morning, I ask myself, would I be satisfied? Would I be happy if tomorrow were my last day? And then when I do wake up in the morning, I say to myself, "This is your last day."

Thinking about that in earnest for five or ten minutes is, I think, at least some sort of preparation for calm on that eventual day—certainly better than never even contemplating the fact that one will die.

I have asked myself this question these last two decades every night before going to sleep. Having kept it up so long, life and death have both come to seem to me to be a kind of dream.

VIII. Waiting for *Tariki* to Blow

Transmitting Shinran's Thought to the People

In recent years, an increasing number of people in the West have begun to show an interest in Buddhism. Perhaps this shows how little trust there is in the economic boom that is driving most of Europe and America.

Perhaps the very ubiquity of "the good life" has made people ask themselves, "How much longer will this last? Will everything disappear tomorrow? Will I be able to live with all the comforts I have begun to feel are my just deserts?"

It seems to me that people are beginning to demonstrate a wish to live in a new way, to explore unexplored dimensions.

Or, from another perspective, it may be a sign that we have entered the global age. Perhaps we realize that it is impossible to live happily in such wealth when others are mired in poverty and backwardness. Perhaps this is the beginning of a search for a new personal accountability.

Just as so many are determined to master the Internet and acquire computer skills in order to compete in the global market, they feel that they should have a religion, as most others in the world do.

I first encountered Rennyo nineteen years ago. I had been a very successful writer but I decided to stop writing altogether to return to university. I just happened to take a Buddhist history course that dealt with Rennyo, treating the organizations called *ko* that he introduced to small villages in the Omi region. I have frequently called Rennyo the Lech Walesa of the Japanese Middle Ages.

Walesa was active throughout Poland as a union leader. He fought against the Communist Party with the Catholic Church in one hand and the self-governing unions in the other. I thought this was very similar to what Rennyo did. During the Onin Rebellion, Rennyo remained in his temple busily writing his *Gobunsho*. At the same time, the monks of the Ji sect were performing a variety of volunteer activities to help those suffering in the rebellion's aftermath.

The attraction of Shinran is the attraction of his relentless logic of philosophy and his faith. In contrast, Rennyo is a mass of contradictions. Yet, he has tremendous attraction as a human being. Precisely because of that personal allure, he was able to accomplish the impossible: He transmitted this pure philosophy of Shinran to the masses.

The Eve of Destruction

I have heard some people ascribe the lack of interest in religion as being a healthy sign for our times. Their reasoning is that in times when religion has real power, when the words of religious leaders reverberate through the culture and many people take refuge in religion, the people are often experiencing the most severe hardship and suffering.

That is true, and was certainly the case in the time from Shinran through Rennyo. Rennyo wrote the first part of his *Gobunsho* in the midst of the Kansho-era famine. In Kyoto alone more than eighty thousand were said to have died of starvation. It was a period of earthquakes, typhoons, and epidemics as well. Farmers' uprisings broke out all over Japan, and the feudal warlords were locked in constant battles among themselves.

Corpses were piled high on both banks of the Kamo River in Kyoto, and people had to hold their noses as they crossed the bridges spanning the river. Only after a heavy rain that washed the corpses downstream could the people of Kyoto breathe a sigh of relief.

Scroll paintings of the period show a man holding a rope behind his back with one hand while he lures a dog with food in the other. People ate everything they could find, and not only dogs; there were many cases of cannibalism as well.

It was a time when life was hell, and a human life was no more valuable than a pebble. At such a time, Rennyo appeared in the world, carrying Shinran's teachings on his back and striding into the midst of his fellow sufferers with the power of a lion.

If we shift our gaze to the present time, both politics and economics are in tremendous upheaval. Further, this upheaval is going on all around the world, and the flames of religious and ethnic conflicts that have their origins in economic injustice, much like the farmers' uprising in Rennyo's time, are burning everywhere. Even worse is the spiritual conflict that is growing increasingly desperate the world over.

We are not at peace. At the end of the twentieth century, we face all sorts of invisible threats, and we find ourselves in much the same place as Rennyo long ago: the eve of destruction.

Valuing Grief

In terms of saving people's souls, today may indeed be the time for Rennyo's philosophy of *hi* (sympathy).

It is a sympathy that weeps at its own helplessness, that cries out, "Why can't I do anything for this person? Am I to watch helplessly as he falls before my very eyes? Why can't I put an end to this tragedy and suffering?"

We must value this kind of sympathy, taught Rennyo.

Since World War II, we Japanese have tried to build a new, rational, "dry" culture on top of our emotional, "wet" native culture. We have succeeded in creating a rational, logical, efficient society, but as a result people's hearts are parched and cracked.

Modern intellectuals despise emotionalism and sentiment, but it has proved impossible to completely reject what lies at the very root of our being.

Yet, that core is even now becoming desiccated.

Political leaders, religious leaders, intellectuals, call for "family values," and "moral education," but their efforts will certainly be for naught.

We should not scorn or fear emotion. The challenge we face is to encourage an emotional richness and the feeling of sympathy as a base for a truly humane education.

This, it seems to me, is the ray of light that the religious leader Rennyo, who was filled with the spirit of sympathy, is sending to illuminate us five hundred years later.

We need to awaken to the tremendous power of Rennyo's sympathy, and when we do, our parched hearts will once again be nourished by the waters of deep feeling.

There Is No Escape from Desire Through Willpower

"Acceptance of one's lot in life" is often thought of as a negative, despairing idea, but it is not really a bad thing.

It means having the wisdom to know what reality is, and the strength to react properly to that reality.

Shinran is an example of the most thoroughgoing acceptance of his time, the Japanese Middle Ages.

What did he accept?

The fact that there is no escape from one's desires and spiritual obstructions through willpower alone.

Shinran engaged in the most rigorous religious practice up to the age of twenty-nine. But no matter what he did, he could not control the burning fires of error and desire. Then he awakened.

"I have awakened to the truth that I cannot awaken by my own power," he said.

In other words, Shinran accepted the fact that he could not attain liberation by his own power.

The True Pure Land order that Shinran founded is based on his teaching of Other Power; it does not tell us to try to get rid of our obstructions and desires. This marks it from the other sects of Japanese Buddhism. In fact, it is different from Buddhism in India and China as well.

It is a religion of true and full acceptance. Because one accepts reality, it becomes clear, and pursuing it with a new clarity one arrives at truth. From there is born a true and quiet strength.

Simply thinking that you can conquer the illness or difficulties that afflict you will not actually solve the problem. It is better to accept the fact that our lives are limited. Be grateful that you are alive now and savor this moment of life. This supple, flexible state of mind will become a great source of strength when you face a crisis.

A supple state of mind is not born from the denial of death. It is born from looking intently at death, looking intently at life, and welcoming them both.

This supple state of mind is what supports a person during a crisis.

Strength is not the only secret to survival.

The Japanese Awareness of Sin Is Deep and Enduring

How many of our fellow human beings have we killed in the twentieth century? Surely we have murdered more of our own species than has any other animal on Earth.

If this is evil, it is an evil that each and every one of us bears. The philosophy of Other Power is based on the conviction that it is impossible to clearly divide people into good and evil, angels and demons. All of us have that evil within our very beings. Shinran said, "We all have deep and heavy evil karma."

This belief that all human beings carry a load of sin, partake of evil by their very nature, has penetrated deeply into the lower classes of Japanese society from the twelfth century on. It is a concept that stands in opposition to the secular, social concept of shame (*haji*).

The idea of shame is the product of the warrior culture, refined over the centuries. In contrast, the concepts of the *nembutsu* and sin run, like groundwater, through the consciousness of the lower classes, who are looked down on by the warriors.

The astonishing thing about Shinran's thought is that he doesn't focus on sin as the shared state of all humanity but as something each individual must awaken to in an intensely personal, one-on-one encounter with the Buddha. The idea that I can be saved by facing, individually, directly, and alone, the absolute truth of the universe in the form of Amida Buddha may superficially resemble the Judeo-Christian contract with God, but it is very different on several scores.

A contract is a mutual agreement between two parties, but Other Power holds that the Buddha draws the individual toward him and holds him by the hand. That is the meaning of "taking refuge" (*kie*) in the Buddha. The big issue in this case is whether the individual can completely yield to the Buddha or not.

A feeling of complete powerlessness is needed here, a disillusionment with the self, disaffection with others, and the feeling that one is, here and now, in hell. The philosophy of Absolute Other Power is the response to this state.

At such a point, any faith in the self disappears without a trace. One may fight with invincible will against illness and win out, but we are all fated to die in the end, of some disease or other. There is no lasting victory. All victories are only temporary, the triumph of a moment.

I try to imagine not a calmness that comes from faith in the self but a gentle composure that comes from faith in the other, but I confess it is beyond me. No doubt I still cling to a smidgeon of trust in my self.

Yet, I still hope that I can live my life not boldly but buoyantly.

Something That All Can Accomplish

The leaders of the *nembutsu* movement in the Kamakura period were concerned with the people they saw before them, the masses who tried desperately to find peace and security in the midst of their sufferings.

Self-Power practices are impossible for such people. They can't all just stop their labors in the world and become monks. Wasn't there some way that they could find the strength to live *as they were*, as laborers, as family members, as those living at society's modest levels?

What all people can do is to reflect on their own lives, realize the depth of their foolishness and desires, and recognize their own evil. From the resulting despair, a way out becomes visible: Other Power. Honen taught "only the *nembutsu,*" and Shinran taught "only faith." Rennyo said that both the *nembutsu* and faith were the beckoning of Other Power. "Only faith" was also the doctrine of Martin Luther, whose religious revolution, the Reformation, was to shake all Europe several hundred years later, in the sixteenth century.

On August 24, 1999, an article by Yoichiro Ikeda appeared in the evening edition of the *Asahi Newspaper.* According to the article, the Roman Catholic and the Lutheran churches were making a joint declaration on the doctrine of Christian justification, the first time they had done so since the sixteenth century. Simply put, the doctrine of justification refers to the act in which God, through the sacrifice of Jesus Christ, forgives a person for his sins and releases him from punishment.

The Catholic Church had, up to this point, always emphasized that we are saved not only by taking refuge in God but also by performing acts of goodness while on Earth. It stressed the importance of religious ceremonies and performing good works.

Martin Luther, in contrast, emphasized that our salvation does not depend upon our good works, religious practice, self-control, charity, or any of the acts we perform in our lives. Salvation is bestowed upon us when we have unwavering faith in God.

The agreement these two sides arrived at on salvation is extremely interesting, because this is one of the most important of all doctrinal issues. When we look closely at this matter, we see it is the issue of Self-Power and Other Power being played out in Christianity.

I Believe Because It Is Irrational

Let us look again at Mr. Ikeda's article in the *Asahi Newspaper*.

Up to now, the Catholic Church had insisted that in addition to deep faith, individual efforts to perform good deeds, engage in religious practice, and control one's desires were prerequisites for salvation.

The Protestant churches, on the other hand, since the Reformation in the sixteenth century, had proclaimed that salvation depended upon faith alone. The priority was faith. This reminds us of the debate among Honen's disciples on the question of the priority of faith or practice.

The debate was settled when Honen silently decided in favor of the priority of faith, the minority position put forth by Shinran.

Shinran believed that the *nembutsu* was important, but first came complete faith in the Buddha. That pure faith was the natural response of a person when the Buddha's light reached out to him and he lifted his face to see it. The *nembutsu* was an utterance of astonishment and emotion, a cry of rejoicing that escaped one's lips at the moment.

It is not a matter of making an effort to find the Buddha and finally discovering him. The Buddha comes looking for you and says, "Hey, here I am. Look, over here!" You only notice his call. This is what Shinran defined as Other Power.

What Buddhists call "thusness" (*shinnyo*, reality just as it is) is the light of the real. The Buddha comes to us from beyond that light, which is why he is also called the Thus-Come One (*nyorai*). The Buddha who walks toward that light is the Thus-Gone One (*nyoko*). The practice of trying to follow the Thus-Gone One, heading toward his back, framed in the light, is the practice of Self-Power.

"I don't have that faith in myself," thought Shinran. "With so much delusion, with such a weak mind, unable to rid myself of desires, foolish and steeped in sin," he chose Other Power.

Mr. Ikeda's article goes on to quote a Protestant minister and religion professor: "Protestants believe that humankind is deeply mired in sin and cannot save itself through its own efforts. We can only be saved by Christ." In other words, they emphasize Other Power. Catholics teach that we are saved not only through the power of Christ but also through good works, in other words a combination of Other Power and Self-Power.

Of course, a brief newspaper article cannot illuminate the fine points of this controversy. The point that deserves our attention, no doubt, is that Protestants and Catholics are now engaged in dialogue on the subject of salvation. This trend toward dialogue has only begun to take concrete form in the twentieth century.

The article continues:

In 1967, the Vatican and the Lutheran church, the largest of the Protestant denominations, with sixty million followers, established an international committee, and from that time a theological dialogue has continued. In June the World Conference of Lutherans and the Vatican's Committee for the Promotion of Christian Doctrinal Unity held a joint news conference and announced that in October they would sign a joint agreement on the doctrine of justification.

The justification will read in part, "Both parties hereby agree that justification is due solely to God's blessing and is not attained by good works. It is received only through faith, and its fruits are manifested through good works."

Can anyone sympathetic to the thought of Shinran fail to be astonished by this declaration? This joint declaration of the Lutheran Church and the Vatican very closely approaches the core of Japan's Other Power Buddhism. If that declaration were reworded as "Salvation (birth in the Pure Land, *ojo*) is due solely to the Buddha's (Amida's) compassion (original vow) and is not attained by good works (miscellaneous practices). It is received only through faith (taking refuge), and its fruits are manifested through acts of gratitude (*nembutsu*)," it would be a perfect expression of the essence of the original vow of Other Power.

The faith described in this joint declaration overlaps considerably with the position of absolute Other Power. It is unconditional surrender to God. That, in my opinion, is the essence of the greatness of Christianity.

The Christian God transcends the human intellect. His intentions cannot be divined with our limited mental faculties. Precisely because he is such a transcendent, ineffable being, he cannot be followed with reason; absolute faith is indispensable.

We believe because we cannot understand; believing because we have evidence or proof belongs to the level of science or commerce.

Shinran said, "Other Power faith takes the unreasonable as its reason." Believing because we understand belongs to the realm of worldly agreements. God can act cruelly, can act unreasonably, but such acts only seem cruel or unreasonable to human reason. That is precisely why we seek unconditional faith.

There Is No Way to Faith Without Encounters with Good People

Religion is a strange thing, and in some ways a cruel thing. How many times have human beings implored their gods, "Why have you forsaken me?" The will of the absolute and only God is unfathomable by human reason and incomprehensible in this world. That is why there is faith in the first place. This is what gives value and meaning to faith.

When Shinran was asked, "Why do you believe that *nembutsu*

will bring you birth in the Pure Land?" he replied, "I am only practicing according to the instructions of a good person." There is no other reason. Honen told me to chant the *nembutsu* and receive Amida Buddha's assistance, and all I have done is believe in him.

There are times when I find the words that follow this statement superfluous. According to Yuien's record, Shinran went on to say, "If Honen's words are false and I, deceived by them, fall into hell, what difference does it make? I cannot save myself through my own efforts anyway, and I was naturally bound for hell as it was. Since I am bound for hell, I won't have the slightest regret if I should end up in hell in spite of my belief in the *nembutsu*."

This statement by Shinran is very famous, but I can't help thinking that Yuien has elaborated somewhat here on Shinran's real utterance.

His earlier statement already fully lays out the principle of faith. There's no need to say anything further.

The "good person" in Shinran's statement could be a teacher, a more experienced person in life, a friend. It doesn't have to be a person of deep faith or knowledge and integrity. It might even be a hideously evil person. Each of us, I think, has his or her own encounter with the "good person" who sets us on the way to faith.

Our encounter with that good person has nothing to do with our efforts or our faith. Some of us never meet that person as long as we live. That's how Other Power works. Not everything can be gained by seeking.

I Feel the Wind of Other Power

Reliance upon the original vow of Other Power is a fundamental step in the path of the Pure Land Buddhist. It means you have moved away from dependence on others. In fact, it begins with abandoning dependence on everything: the nation, the constitution, the government, hospitals, schools, businesses, moral and intellectual leaders of the world, the mass media, the banks. Abandon dependence, too, on your family, spouse, parents, children. The original vow of Other Power means recognizing one's true Self Power.

Over the years, I have come to think of the invisible power that gives one the courage to be fully independent as Other Power, and the original vow as the life force of the universe.

All religions, belief systems, and objects of worship—whether gods or Buddhas, Christianity, Hinduism, Islam, Confucianism or Taoism, the native religions of various localities, nature worship, and indeed all intercourse with unseen realms of existence—have at the root, a quiet resonance with Other Power.

A society without such a religion or spiritual culture, whatever form it may take, is a weak and empty society.

Without some relationship to the divine, it would be very difficult for an individual to even possess an identity, much less control his own destiny. Instead we are locked in a hall of mirrors, buffeted about by hot airs of desire, greed, and pride.

Today, as we stand on the threshold of a period of great upheaval, we see signs of a new recognition of spiritual values. To me it seems to be the first breeze of the wind of Other Power.

I hope my readers will feel that even the fact that they are reading these rough and random thoughts of mine is a manifestation of Other Power. I hope that they are open to its healing winds, its shining lights.

The Invisible Power That Supports Our Lives

We do not exist solely on the material plane. We are also spiritual beings, and our souls require sustenance.

We need love.

We need a purpose in life.

We need friendship.

We need the challenge of work.

We need to feel connected to family and relations.

I think just living the first week of life is an amazing accomplishment. Then we go on to live ten months, three years, ten years, twenty years—what a vast, invisible support system keeps us alive! How hard our life works to support our existence!

Some people may be blessed with superior strengths or abilities. There are those who possess wonderful natural athletic abilities. Others are brilliant mathematicians. Others may have tremendous physical energy and courage. Still others may be marvelously creative. Others may be strong willed.

Such people may attempt and achieve great things, winning the applause of their fellow human beings, but they should by no means pride themselves on their accomplishments. Rather, they should be humble and grateful that they have been blessed with more energy, more good fortune than others.

I believe that all people, even if they accomplish nothing in their lives, or appear to be accomplishing nothing, are engaged in a tremendous struggle simply to be.

I also believe that every person born into this world, even an evil one, is here because he has a role to play in life. It was Shakespeare who said, "The world's a stage." On a stage there are heroes and there are irredeemable villains, there are faithful friends and there are traitors.

No matter what we do, no matter what our dreams, how much

love we have to give, or how creative or clever we are, no matter how much we devote ourselves to others, our lives here on Earth are limited. In that time we inevitably age, we fall ill, and we die. All that is determined from the start, at the very moment we are born.

We are all travelers who, from our first wail at birth, are making a journey, one step at a time, toward death. Knowing life's end, how meaningless it is to compare oneself to others, and harboring feelings of either inferiority or superiority.

Although we know what fate awaits us, we do not succumb to despair but dare to live.

Given the circumstances, what a great and important feat that is!

Art work by Reiko Itsuki

Glossary

Akunin Shoki. "Evil people are the proper object of salvation." This doctrine states that the Buddha's compassion is directed first and foremost at those who seem beyond it, that is, those who are unable to lift themselves out of their state of evil and suffering through their own efforts. So-called good people, who can make an effort to save themselves through Buddhist practice, are, relatively speaking, only the secondary object of the Buddha's saving power.

Endo, Shusaku (1923–98). Popular Catholic novelist and playwright; humorist. Born in Tokyo, Endo lived in China as a child and returned to Japan with his mother in 1933 after his parents' divorce. A Catholic aunt persuaded him to be baptized at the age of eleven. Endo, who majored in French literature at Keio University, went to France in 1950, the first Japanese to study abroad since World War II. Soon after his return to Japan, Endo began writing fiction. Some of his works include *Shiroi Hito* (White man, 1955), which received the Akutagawa Prize, and the Noma Literary Prize–winning *Samurai* (1980; tr. *The Samurai,* 1982). During his career, he also edited *Mita Bungaku,* a prestigious literary journal, and was an active member in a number of literary organizations.

Esoteric Buddhism (*mikkyo,* literally "the secret teachings"). Also known as *himitsu Bukkyo,* or "secret Buddhism." A special tradition within Buddhism stemming from the belief that the most profound doctrines of Buddhism are to be kept secret, not expounded publicly. The word "secret" also refers to the mystical character of these teachings. Although the origins of this school can be traced back to the early days of Buddhism, the seventh-century Indian monk Nagarjuna is traditionally known as its founder. *Mikkyo* was brought from China to Japan by Kukai, whose teachings form the basis of the Shingon sect.

Gobunsho. A collection of eighty letters in five volumes by Rennyo, edited by his disciple

Ennyo, to Rennyo's followers, explaining the faith in the *nembutsu* and Other Power in simple, accessible language. The Honganji sect refers to them as the *Gobunsho*, and the Otani sect calls them the *Ofumi*.

Honen (1133–1212, real name Genku). Buddhist priest and founder of the Jodo sect who spearheaded the Kamakura Buddhist "reformation." The son of a samurai, Honen entered the Buddhist order at age eight after the death of his father. After mastering the doctrines of the Tendai sect at the temple Enryakuji on Mount Hiei, he came to the realization that *nembutsu* was the only way to achieve *ojo*, rebirth in Amida's Pure Land. Honen was laicized and exiled for his role in the movement by the Buddhist establishment in Kyoto. He was finally allowed to return to Kyoto in 1211, just a few months before his death.

Igyo. Easy practice. Buddhist practice that can be carried out by anyone, as opposed to advanced study or difficult meditation and visualization practices. It is usually used to refer to the *nembutsu*.

Jinen Honi. This expression means "everything is just as it is in accord with the Dharma," or "reality just as it is." Shinran used this concept to express the idea that we are all saved by the Buddha just as we are, when we abandon our own efforts to achieve salvation and accept the saving power of the Buddha.

Jodo sect (Jodoshu). School of Pure Land Buddhism founded by Honen, known for its advocacy of *nembutsu* for the purpose of *ojo*. The first of the new Buddhist sects to emerge in the late Heian period (794–1185), it remains the second largest after its independent subsect, the Jodo Shin sect. The founding of the Jodo sect is traditionally dated to 1175, the year Honen left his mountain hermitage and descended to the capital of Heiankyo (now Kyoto) to preach the selective or exclusive practice of *nembutsu*. Although in the Edo period (1600–1868) the influence of Shinran's understanding of the Pure Land as an ever-present state of grace came to be felt, the Jodo sect largely retained its original abhorrence of the world and desire for the pure beyond.

Jodo Shin sect (Jodo Shinshu; often called the True Pure Land sect). One of the traditional thirteen schools of Japanese Buddhism and a major form of Pure Land Buddhism. Its founder, Shinran, used the term Jodo Shinshu to denote the "true essence" of Pure Land teaching as expounded by his teacher Honen, but the term later came to designate the sect that evolved around Shinran's teachings. According to Shinran, the Pure Land tradition originated in the Original Vow of the Amida Buddha to save all mankind, especially in a time when human degradation becomes manifest in ineffectual religious practices, spiritual bankruptcy, brutish egoism, and social chaos. The Jodo Shin sect became one of the most influential Buddhist movements, especially among the masses. During the Edo period, the sect secured a permanent place in society.

Kamo no Chomei (1155–1216). A poet and essayist best known for a brief work, *Hojoki* (Tale of a ten-foot-square hut). At about the age of fifty he retired from the secular world and took up residence in a little pilgrim's hut away in the mountains. He also composed a work on poetic theory, the *Mumyo Sho,* and a collection of Buddhist fables, the *Hosshin Shu.*

Kie. To take refuge. Taking refuge means to commit oneself to the Buddha, the Dharma (the teachings of the Buddha), and the Samgha (the Buddhist religious community). It is the first step along the way of Buddhism practice and a term common to all schools of Buddhism.

Kukai (774–835, also known as Kobo Daishi). Buddhist priest of the early Heian period (794–1185); founder of the Shingon sect of Buddhism. He was born into a declining aristocratic family at Byobugaura in Sanuki province in Shikoku. At age eighteen he entered the national college in the capital with the aim of becoming a statesman but withdrew after a few years. Kukai then pursued his Buddhist studies while wandering about the country as an itinerant hermit practicing meditation. In 804 he sailed to China as a student monk and returned to Japan in 806 as a master of esoteric Buddhist teachings. Credited with the invention of the *kana* syllabary, Kukai is considered the father of Japanese culture. He was also known as a poet, calligrapher, sculptor, and lexicographer who compiled the *Tenrei Bansho Meigi,* the oldest extant dictionary in Japan.

Nembutsu. The invocation of "Namu Amida Butsu," uttered in the hope of rebirth into Amida's Pure Land. This modern conception of *nembutsu* was popularized by Honen in the twelfth century. In 1175, Honen asserted the independence of the Pure Land movement and taught that the simple utterance of the Buddha's name was the best path to salvation. The Jodo sect and the Jodo Shin sect took *nembutsu* as their primary religious exercise.

Ocho. "To move sideways and leap to enlightenment." One of the categories into which Shinran divided the Buddhist teachings. He uses it to refer to the sudden enlightenment (a leap) attained through absolute faith in the vow of Amida Buddha. He calls it "moving sideways" in contrast to another category, "moving upward," which he uses to describe the process of moving upward through levels of Buddhist practice to attain enlightenment. In contrast, moving sideways implies moving to enlightenment just as we are, with all our imperfections.

Ojo. Birth in the Pure Land. *Ojo* has been interpreted in various ways in different sects of

Buddhism. The popular understanding is to be born in the Pure Land of Amitabha Buddha after death, although Shinran and others insist that this "birth" takes place in life, when one awakens to absolute faith in the power of the Buddha.

Prince Shotoku (574–622, Shotoku Taishi). Statesman of the Asuka period (593–710); second son of Emperor Yomei. As regent for the empress Suiko, Prince Shotoku instituted the *Kan'i Junikai* ("twelve cap ranks") and the Seventeen-Article Constitution to strengthen imperial authority.

Qu Yuan (ca. 340 B.C.–ca. 278 B.C.). A political leader and poet of the Chu dynasty of China in the Warring States period. He was active in government but lost his post through the slander of rivals and, after a period of wandering, committed suicide by drowning.

Rennyo (1415–1499, also known as Rennyo Kenju). Buddhist priest and eighth *hossu* (head abbot) of the Honganji temple. Under his leadership, Honganji grew to become the unchallenged center of Shinshu (the Jodo Shin sect) and the largest, most powerful religious organization in late-medieval Japan. Rennyo sought temporary refuge in various locations when the Tendai sect of Enryakuji sent armed forces of monk warriors to destroy Honganji. In 1471, Rennyo moved his base to Yoshizaki (now Fukui Prefecture), where he perfected and disseminated the *Ofumi* (Letters), his principal contribution to Shinshu literature. In concise, easily understandable vernacular language, Rennyo set forth the essence of Shinran's teaching of salvation through faith in the Amida Buddha and vigorously attacked the various heresies he encountered.

Saeki, Join (1867–1952). Join Saeki entered the Hosso School at Horyuji temple in Nara at the age of six and began to apprentice as a monk. He took the tonsure in 1873 and in 1894 he graduated from Nara Teachers College. He became head monk of Horyuji in 1903, and remained so for more than forty years. In 1950 he left the Hosso School and founded a new temple, Shotokuji.

Shinran (1173–1263). Founder of the Jodo Shin sect of Pure Land Buddhism, a sect based on the principle of birth into the Pure Land through faith alone. Shinran entered the monastic life at about age eight and served as a *doso* (menial monk) at the temple of Enryakuji on Mount Hiei until he became a disciple of Honen in 1201. As Honen's *nembutsu* group became popular and influential, criticism and opposition led to government abolition of the community and Shinran was exiled to Echigo Province for four years. From his return to Kyoto around 1235 until about 1260, Shinran devoted himself to literary efforts. The central thesis of Shinran's teaching developed from his deep awareness of the inadequacy of the individual, self-motivated efforts to achieve enlightenment in the face of profound and persistent egoism, and the ineradicability of passion.